THE JEWS AND THE POLES
IN WORLD WAR II

THE JEWS AND THE POLES IN WORLD WAR II

Stefan Korbonski

HIPPOCRENE BOOKS

New York

For information, address: Hippocrene Books, Inc.
171 Madison Avenue, New York, NY 10016

Library of Congress Cataloging-in-Publication Data

Korboński, Stefan.
  The Jews and the Poles in World War II / Stefan Korboński.
  Includes index.
  ISBN 0-87052-591-3
  1. Jews—Poland—Persecutions. 2. Holocaust, Jewish (1939–
1945)—Poland. 3. World War, 1939–1945—Jews—Rescue—Poland.
4. World War, 1939–1945—Underground movements, Jewish—
Poland. 5. Holocaust survivors—Poland. 6. Poland—Ethnic
relations. I. Title.
DS135.P6K55 1989
940.53'18'09438—dc20   89-7439
                                                             CIP

CONTENTS

Introduction

The charges leveled by the Jews against the Poles for allegedly sharing responsibility for the Holocaust by not preventing the slaughter of the Jews by the Nazis are groundless, unfair, and slanderous. An individual or a nation can be blamed for denying help which could be given, but not for failing to do the impossible.

The fact that the Poles were utterly powerless to stop the extermination of the Jews was attested by the messages entrusted in 1942 to the underground courier Jan Karski and addressed to the Allied leaders by two prominent representatives of the Polish Jews, Adolph Berman and Leon Feiner. They were both living outside the ghetto and were sheltered by Polish friends. They wrote:

> We want you to tell to the Polish government in London and to the Allied governments and leaders that we are completely defenseless in the face of the German criminals. We cannot save ourselves, nor can anyone else in Poland save us. The Polish underground resistance can save a few of us, but not the masses. The Germans do not plan to subordinate us, as they do other nations. We are being systematically exterminated; our community will be totally destroyed. A few may be saved, but the three million Polish Jews are doomed.
>
> Neither a Jewish nor a Polish resistance can do anything to stop the slaughter. Make the Allied powers responsible for what is hap-

pening. Let no Allied leader be able to pretend that he did not know that we are being wiped out and that the only help can come from outside.

The impossibility of helping the Jews was confirmed by the numerous German ordinances imposing the death penalty for any assistance rendered to the Jews and by the many Polish families summarily executed on the spot when they were found to be sheltering Jews.

The Jewish Historic Institute in Warsaw confirmed in 1968 the cases of 343 Christian Poles murdered by the Germans for helping Jews, and many other cases are under investigation.

Despite these documented facts, the campaign of slander against the Poles continues in full force, sometimes reaching absurdity. "Wladka," a woman who took part in the ghetto rising, accused the Poles in print, stating that "the Danes saved their Jews, but the Poles did not." She forgot to mention that there were 6,000 Jews in Denmark and 3,500,000 in Poland, or that the Danes sent their Jews by boat to nearby neutral Sweden, while Poland had no outlet to the free world.

My position as the last surviving leader of the Polish Underground State during the German occupation compels me to place on record the truth by reporting how we saved as many Polish Jews as was possible. Of the 6,000 Yad Vashem medals awarded in Israel for saving Jews during the Holocaust, 2,000 were given to Christian Poles; but even that figure does not reflect the scale of the efforts which could not achieve the impossible, but did save thousands.

It is my hope that the facts related here may help to clear the clouded atmosphere of Polish-Jewish relations.

CHAPTER I

The Jews' Asylum in Poland

THE KINGDOM OF ISRAEL WAS ESTABLISHED TOWARD THE END OF the eleventh century before Christ. During the first century A.D., when Israel was a colony of Rome, the Jews rebelled against the Romans (A.D. 66). In A.D. 70, Emperor Titus deported Jews to parts of the Roman Empire, notably Gaul, Pannonia, and Iberia. The defeat of the second Jewish uprising in A.D. 132–135, under Simon Bar-Kochba, ended in the expulsion from Israel of the remaining Jews, initiating the era of the diaspora—that is, the dispersion of the Jews first into Europe and then throughout the world. The Talmud, a Jewish religious and legal code, was developed during the Exile in Babylon and has been guiding the life of the Jews ever since. In the eighth century the first Jews reached the regions of Ruthenia and Poland. Starting with the twelfth century, restrictions aimed at the

1

Jews began to be enforced in most countries of western Europe. They included the prohibition of owning land or practicing trades reserved for the guilds. Thus, Jews were confined to separate quarters or streets. They were allowed, however, to lend money and practice usury. In the twelfth to the fifteenth centuries persecution began, particularly at the time of the Crusades. Jews were expelled from England in 1290, from France in 1306 and 1394, from Spain in 1492, from Portugal in 1496–1497. They were also expelled at various times from the many duchies of Germany.

During the time of the expulsions, the Jews sought asylum in Poland, which became the home of most of the Jews and the principal center of Jewish culture. The Jews settled in Poland because it was the country which offered them the best conditions of life. Their status was determined by the successive charters of Boleslaw the Pious in 1264 and Casimir the Great in 1334, 1354, and 1367.

Toward the end of his life, Casimir the Great took a Jewish mistress by the name of Esther, who was said to have obtained privileges for the Jews. She had two sons by him: Niemir and Pelka, who were generously provided for in the king's will.

The royal charters made of the Jews a separate estate, similar to those of the gentry, the burghers, and the peasants. The Jews had their own boroughs, governed by a council called "Kahal," and their own courts of law. They enjoyed the full protection of the law and the right of practicing trades, a right denied them in western Europe. They also had the right to conduct banking operations and grant loans, to become lessees of mills and inns owned by the squires, and to be franchised as tax collectors for the state.

The decline of the cities in the eighteenth century caused an exodus to rural areas, where the Jews monopolized the country inns and taverns. The character of Yankel in Mickiewicz's great epic poem *Pan Tadeusz* remains the archetype of a Jewish tavern keeper, presented by the author with affection.

Prior to the partitions of Poland by Russia, Prussia, and Austria in 1772, 1793, and 1795, the Jews constituted 7 percent of

Poland's population (28 percent of the population of towns). In the war of Poland against Russia in 1794, the Jews responded to the appeal of Thaddeus Kosciuszko and enlisted. Berek Yoselevich formed a Jewish cavalry regiment under his command.

In the sovereign Polish-Lithuanian Commonwealth, prior to the partitions, the Jews enjoyed extensive autonomy and more freedom than anywhere else in the world. They formed their own settlements within a city, with synagogues, ritual baths called "mikvas," ritual slaughterhouses, schools called "cheders," and rabbinical colleges.

There were two branches of the Judaic faith: Chassidic and Sabataite. Renowned holy rabbis called "cadyks" held court in places such as Sadogira, Bobowa, Kozienice, and Lublin. The rabbinical colleges, called "yeshibots," taught mainly the Talmud and Old Testament, and were attended also by Jews from other countries. The most famous among the rabbinical colleges were those of Krakow and Lublin.

Small towns gradually acquired Jewish majorities of population. Emigrants from such small towns attained positions of distinction, as, for example, the Baruchs from Chodziez, Admiral Hyman Rickover from a village near Warsaw, or the first head of Israel, David Ben-Gurion, from Plonsk. The Jews, who used Yiddish among themselves and broken Polish when communicating with the Poles, were mainly shopkeepers, tailors, shoemakers, milkmen, bakers, and artisans in other trades.

The Jews in Partitioned Poland

The situation of the Jews deteriorated considerably under the rule of Russia, Prussia, and Austria, in their respective parts of Poland. They numbered 1,271,000 in the Russian section, 50,000 in the Prussian, and 800,000 in the Austrian, for a total of 2,121,000. The Russian government imposed many restrictions on the Jews, while the Prussians and Austrians tried to germanize them.

Tsar Alexander I promulgated a Jewish statute under which the Jews were forbidden residence in the rural areas of Russia proper and were not allowed to attend state schools, wear gaberdines and yarmulkes, or speak Hebrew or Yiddish. They were compelled to speak only Russian. In 1827 Tsar Nicholas I ordered more Jews to be drafted for military service. However, Tsar Alexander II allowed his deputy in Poland, the Margrave Wielopolski, to allow some concessions to the Jews, such as the right to acquire land and real estate. Some Jews took part in the Polish uprising against Russia in 1863, and as a result most of their rights were canceled. On the other hand, the concessions obtained by Wielopolski, who was Polish, as well as the fact that both the Poles and the Jews were oppressed by Russia, brought the two closer together and contributed to some assimilation by Polish Jews.

In Russia proper, after the attempted assassination of Tsar Alexander II in 1881, reprisals and pogroms of Jews became common. The word *pogrom*, which is purely Russian, described the actions of Russians. It later acquired wider currency, but was often used inaccurately. The Russian government started the forcible deportation of Jews from Russia to Russian-occupied Poland. The arrival of the "Litvaks," who spoke Russian, was not welcomed by the Polish Jews. However, the Russian Jews were eventually reluctantly absorbed.

In the part of Poland under Prussia, King Frederick II ordered the deportation of poor Jews. Anyone unable to prove assets of at least three hundred thalers was expelled, and the remaining Jews were compelled to speak only German. The poor Jews moved to Poland, which was under Russian rule.

In the part of Poland under the Hapsburg Austrian Empire, Emperor Joseph II declared in 1789 the so-called Tolerance Act, which granted to the Jews the freedom of religion and trade, while retaining the prohibition of selling liquors and leasing land, mills, and tolls. Furthermore, the Jews were forced to accept German names assigned to them by the authorities. Only in 1867, when the absolute Hapsburg monarchy was converted into the constitutional Austro-Hungarian Empire, was equality of all citizens granted regardless of faith or origin. The part of Poland under Austrian rule, called Galicia, obtained a degree of autonomy; and its legislature, elected in 1868, abolished all the restrictions against the Jews. Assimilation was thus accelerated, and in 1910, 925 out of a thousand Jews in Galicia described themselves as Poles.

In the meantime, both Jewish and non-Jewish Poles emigrated to the United States in increasing numbers.

CHAPTER II

The Jews in Independent Poland (1918–1939)

THE DAY OF NOVEMBER 11, 1918, WAS ACCEPTED AS THE DATE OF Poland's recovered independence. The Austrian empire had already collapsed, Russia was in the throes of revolution, and the German troops still in Poland were disarmed on that day. Political leadership was assumed by Joseph Pilsudski, the commander of the Polish Legion formed under Austrian rule; he was a former socialist. Pilsudski appointed a cabinet headed by a socialist, Moraczewski. On November 28, 1918, the government enacted an electoral law which established a fully democratic system with universal, equal, and secret voting for all citizens. The first election was held on January 26, 1919. Three hundred forty members of parliament were elected, including ten Jews who formed the Jewish Caucus, headed by Isaac Grunbaum. At its third session, on February 20, the Seym (parliament) elected Joseph Pilsudski head of the state and adopted the Provisional Constitution, preliminary to the Constitution of March 17, 1921, which restricted the executive and granted extensive powers to the Seym. The Seym was overthrown by Pilsudski's coup of May 1926.

The euphoria which greeted Poland's new independence after over a century of alien occupation was not shared by all the Jewish citizens, who still lived by the dream of "next year in Jerusalem" and regarded themselves as residents in the diaspora, now Polish instead of Russian, Prussian, or Austrian. The situation of the Jews, however, was significantly improved. They again enjoyed full freedom, as they did in the prepartition of Poland. They formed their own communities, speaking Yiddish, wearing gaberdines, yarmulkes, beards, and liturgical attire on their religious feasts. They observed strictly the rules of the Talmud and ancient customs, such as tossing sins on a river to be washed away.

The eminent Zionist leader Jabotinsky wrote in his book *The Jewish State*, published in Warsaw in 1937: "We formed the ghettos ourselves, voluntarily, for the same reason for which Europeans in Shanghai establish their separate quarter, to be able to live together in their own way." Thus, two distinct nationalities lived side by side in Poland for seven centuries without penetrating one another or interfering with one another's way of life.

The Jewish population, which grew faster than the Polish one, was concentrated mainly in towns. Among the larger cities the percentage of Jews was as follows: Bialystok 43; Stanislawow 41.4; Lodz 33.5; Lwow 31.9; Warsaw 30.1; Wilno 28.2; Krakow 25.8.

The percentage of Jews in the smaller towns was even higher. The average percentage of Jews in towns was as follows: Lublin province 49.9; Wolyn province 49.1; Polesie province 49.8.

In small towns the Jews were the majority and the Christian Poles a small minority. In Miedzyrzecz Podlaski, for example, with a total population of 18,000, there were 16,000 Jews and 2,000 Gentiles.

In pre-war Poland there were 130 Yiddish and Hebrew periodicals; 15 Yiddish language theaters; 266 elementary, 12 high school, and 14 vocational schools using Yiddish or Hebrew. While the Jews constituted 49 percent of all lawyers and 46 percent of all doctors, and made up 59 percent of Poland's population engaged in commerce and 21 percent in industry, the majority of Jews, especially those living in eastern Poland, were—like their Polish neighbors—extremely poor because of the slow recovery of Poland's economy, further devastated by the worldwide recession of the early 1930s.

There was a massive increase in the Jewish population in the years 1919–1920, when about 600,000 Russian Jews, fleeing the "white" armies of Generals Denikin and Wrangel, sought asylum in Poland. In 1926 Marshal Pilsudski, a philosemite and former socialist, granted the Jews Polish citizenship with full equality of rights.

Also, assimilation was making progress mainly in the part of Poland formerly annexed by the Hapsburg empire known as Galicia. Jews with a higher education joined professions, and many of them acquired prominence in industry, banking, and finance. They regarded themselves as Poles, even patriots, and ignored their Jewish background, bringing their children up in Polish culture and sometimes not admitting to them their ancestry. Mixed marriages were common in that class, mainly between the daughters of wealthy Jewish businessmen and the sons of impoverished Polish gentry. Many of the Poles of Jewish descent played important roles in various areas of Polish life and made major contributions, fully recognized by their Gentile countrymen.

They were received with open arms by the Polish society, which saw in them Poles by choice rather than by accident of birth. The overwhelming majority of the Jewish population, however, retained their separate identity as Polish citizens of Jewish nationality.

The Jewish family of Kronenberg, using the title of baron,

achieved prominence in the nineteenth century, when Poland was still under the rule of the three partition powers. The rise of the family was started by Leopold Kronenberg, born in Warsaw in 1812, who made a fortune by operating a virtual monopoly of tobacco products in Poland. Kronenberg entered the circle of Polish aristocracy and joined the Agricultural Society. He was opposed at first to the uprising of 1863, but later supported its leader, Langiewicz. After the defeat of the uprising, he founded in 1870 the Bank of Commerce and then, together with J. Wertheim and J. Toeplitz, the Sugar Mills Company and the Coal Mine and Smelters Company. He also founded the Academy of Commerce. During World War II the descendents of that prominent Polish family participated in the Polish Underground State of the resistance against the German invaders.

The Rotwand and Wawelberg families also played important roles in the development of Polish finance and industry. They founded in 1895 the Wawelberg School of Technology.

The Natanson family distinguished itself in the fields of science and culture, while the brothers Maurice and Samuel Orgelbrand were active in printing and publishing. They produced in the years 1859–1868 the 28-volume Polish Encyclopaedia.

Polish literature and culture owe much to Mieczyslaw Grydzewski, who founded, together with Anthony Borman, the weekly *Literary News*, the leading intellectual periodical in Warsaw between 1924 and 1939. They continued its publication in London until the eighties, carrying the torch of Polish culture in exile. Among Grydzewski's close collaborators was Anthony Slonimski, the poet and essayist, whose father Stanislaw, a physician, sheltered Joseph Pilsudski in 1905–1906 when he was sought by the tsar's political police. His brother, Piotr, also a doctor, was a member of the Polish underground resistance during World War II.

Another outstanding Polish writer of Jewish origin was Jozef Wittlin. Together with two poets—Jan Lechon and Casimir Wierzynski—they were in the forties and fifties of our century the bearers of the great tradition of Polish writers dedicated to the cause of independence, even while in exile.

Wilhelm Feldman, a writer and literary critic, joined the group headed by Joseph Pilsudski in 1905 and then enlisted in Pilsudski's "Legion" in 1914 to fight for a free Poland.

Marian Hemar was a poet and satirist who enjoyed great popularity in Poland between 1918 and 1939. He became, during the war and after in London, the bard of the Poles in exile. His patriotic poems broadcast from London by the BBC sustained the spirits of the people of Poland and the Poles scattered throughout the world. When Israel became independent, Hemar was invited there for poetry readings and was welcomed enthusiastically, even though he opened his appearance with a dramatic poem in which he declared that he chose Poland as his motherland and would remain loyal to it until he died.

In an homage to Hemar in a Polish newspaper in London, Piskozub wrote: "I love Hemar as a poet, author of lyrics for songs, satirist and Pole of Mosaic faith. That term 'Poles of Mosaic faith' became familiar in my schooldays, when our teachers: Samuel Wagman, Miriam Lichtman, and classmates: Adam Aibel, Oscar Haker, Joseph Silberstein and Jacob Engelstein, used it to describe themselves. They were all wonderful friends, especially Mundek Hafner, who used to visit me when I was sick in bed and brought his violin to cheer me up with music. I admired Oscar for his essays on Polish literature. Our professor Roman Kobierski collected them as excellent studies. All of the people I named here died at the hands of the Germans."

Julius Kleiner, Boleslaw Lesmian, Julius Klaczko, and Julian Tuwim have well-established positions in the history of Polish literature. Alexander Kraushar, an eminent historian, took part in the Polish uprising of 1863, when he was twenty. In the period between the two wars (1918–1939) his venerable figure could be seen on the streets of Warsaw in the uniform of the rebels of 1863, who were all given officer rank in independent Poland.

Marceli Handelsman, a historian of another generation and professor at Warsaw University, was a member of the Democratic

Party. During World War II he worked in the Polish underground in the information office of the Home Army. He was arrested by the Gestapo and sent to the Gross-Rosen concentration camp.

Joseph Feldman, son of Wilhelm, upheld the family tradition. He was a professor at the Jagiellonian University of Krakow. To evade the Gestapo, he had to assume the name of Sokolowski. Feldman taught at the clandestine Polish university and took part in the Warsaw rising of 1944. After the war he returned to the Krakow university.

Szymon Aszkenazy was another eminent Polish historian; he served as the delegate of Poland to the League of Nations in 1920–1923.

Artur Rubinstein was the most outstanding of the many Polish musicians of Jewish origin. After playing the national anthem of the United States at the inaugural session of the United Nations in San Francisco in 1945, he rose and said: "The seats reserved for the representatives of my country are empty and no one will speak here for Poland. Yet, to recall her struggle and her rights, I will now play the Polish national anthem." The vast audience, including President Harry Truman, rose and listened in silence to the "Dabrowski Mazurka," which is Poland's national anthem. It was all outside the official program, and only an artist of Rubinstein's standing could dare to break protocol in this manner.

Rubinstein, who was raised by Polish aristocrats, loved Poland and expressed his affection in *My Young Years,* his autobiography. He thought Polish women to be the most beautiful and the Polish public the most musically sophisticated and appreciative, which caused him to suffer much stage fright when playing in Poland.

After the Second World War Rubinstein always kept in touch with Polish émigrés. When he visited his native city of Lodz after the war, he commented: "The Poles are crazy people. They restore historic buildings and live themselves in ruins and cellars."

Roman Kramsztyk was one of Poland's outstanding artists.

Confined to the Warsaw ghetto, where he died in 1942, he produced a series of sketches of that tragic scene. He was also the author of a striking portrait of the poet Lechon. Among other notable artists of Jewish extraction were also Henry Kuna, a sculptor and professor of art at Wilno University, Maurice Gotlieb, and Eugene Zak.

Arnold Szyfman was called the father of the Polish theater. He was instrumental in the erection in 1912 of the modern "Polski" theater in Warsaw. After World War I he was successively the founder and director of the "Maly" and "Kameralny" theaters, general director of Warsaw theaters with the addition of the "Narodowy," "Letni," and "Nowy." After World War II he directed the restoration of the Opera House and established in its building a museum of the theater.

In medicine, Professor Ludwik Hirszfeld, the inventor of the system of classifying blood types and the author of many innovative medical works, won world renown. During the German occupation he escaped from the ghetto and was sheltered by Polish families. After the war he taught microbiology at the University of Wroclaw. In addition to writing hundreds of scientific papers, he wrote the *History of One Life* in which he described his eventful war years and the help extended to the Jews by Polish Gentiles.

Leon Berenson was an eminent jurist who defended in tsarist courts in 1905–1908 the Polish revolutionaries of the Polish Socialist Party, of which Pilsudski was a member at the time. Berenson defended Montwill-Mirecki and Henryk Baron, who were sentenced to death and hanged at the Citadel of Warsaw. In 1907–1910 Berenson was a member of a group of political defense counsels. After the war, in 1931–1932, he defended members of parliament, including Herman Lieberman, who were arrested and tried for opposition against Marshal Pilsudski. Berenson died in the Warsaw ghetto on April 22, 1943, leaving in his will an instruction to the Jews to erect after the war a monument of gratitude to the Poles who smuggled food to the ghetto. The monument was to be in the form of a loaf of bread standing upright on a marble foundation.

In the world of finance, the leading personality was probably Alfred Falter, the principal shareholder of the coal and steel consortium "Wspolnota Interesow" in Silesia, as well as its subsidiary, "Robur," owner of about ten coal freighters. Shortly before the war he also gained control of the Bank of Commerce in Warsaw. Falter left Poland immediately after the German attack and accompanied Sikorski's government in exile to London, where he was appointed its vice-minister of finance. When the German government impounded the Robur ships in neutral ports, as the property of the Polish government, the Polish underground secured for Falter legal documents proving that he was the owner of the Robur corporation and managed to get the ships to London. The neutral governments then released the ships to Falter as private property. They were promptly chartered by the Allies, and Falter became the major and perhaps only taxpayer of the Polish government in exile.

Michael Lewin was a well-known businessman, owner of the Silesian Electric Corporation and also the luxury hotel "Jurata" on the Baltic coast. In March 1919 Jerzy Osmolowski, appointed by Pilsudski administrator of the eastern territories under dispute between Poland and the Soviet Union, sent Lewin a cable from Wilno appealing for help because "Wilno was starving." Lewin purchased two railroad trains full of provisions. Riding in the caboose, he delivered them personally to Osmolowski. A few years before the war Lewin used his connections in France to secure a loan of millions of francs for Poland. The loan was finalized during a visit in Paris by Marshal Rydz-Smigly, Pilsudski's successor as commander-in-chief.

While Alfred Falter and Michael Lewin were active in Silesia, Oscar Kon, Nathan Eitingon, and K. Poznanski dominated the textile industries of Lodz, Poland's "Manchester." Each owned factories employing many thousands of workers and belonged to the very small group of Polish millionaires of international standing. It was because of them that Lodz became the "Jewish Promised Land"—the title of a novel by the Polish Nobel laureate Wladyslaw Reymont.

The Polish Socialist Party (PPS), founded in 1892, played an important role in Poland's political life in the period between the wars. Several of its prominent leaders and members of parliament were of Jewish origin, for example: Felix Perl, Herman Lieberman, Herman Diamand, Adam Pragier, and Lydia Ciolkosz.

Felix Perl was one of the founders of the PPS. He went abroad in 1892, was jailed by the tsarist authorities during 1904–1905, became in 1924 the chairman of the central executive committee of the Socialist Party, and served as a member of parliament.

Herman Lieberman was a member of the Austrian parliament in Vienna in 1907–1918. He served in Pilsudski's Legion during World War I; but after the Pilsudski coup of 1926, he joined the opposition and was imprisoned in the fortress of Brzesc. Sentenced to three years' imprisonment, he escaped to Czechoslovakia and in 1941 became the minister of justice in Sikorski's government in exile.

Herman Diamand was also a member of the Austrian parliament in the years 1907–1918. He became a member of the Polish parliament in 1919–1930 and was chairman of the council of the PPS in 1928–1931.

Adam Pragier joined the PPS in 1905, served in the Pilsudski Legion in World War I, and was a member of the Polish parliament in 1922–1930 in opposition to Pilsudski. He was arrested at the same time as Lieberman and then escaped secretly abroad. During World War II he served as minister of information in the Sikorski government in exile in London.

Lydia Ciolkosz worked together with her husband Adam, one of the PPS leaders, as a politician in her own right. She is living in London as one of the leaders of the PPS in exile.

In the Seym and senate, two important but different roles were played by Stanislaw Stronski, Senator Boleslaw Motz, and Senator Stanislaw Posner.

Stronski was in 1913–1914 a member of the Galician parliament, in 1922–1927 a member of the Polish Seym (in the right-wing Christian-National Party), and in 1928–1935 a member of parliament representing the equally rightist National Party. A prominent editor and journalist and an adversary of Pilsudski and his faction, Stronski was in 1939–1943 vice-premier and minister of information in the government in exile of General Sikorski.

Boleslaw Motz, arrested for his part in the 1905 revolution in Russia and deported to Siberia, managed to escape and establish in Paris a medical practice patronized by international millionaires. Though a resident of Paris, he was elected senator in independent Poland and commuted regularly to Warsaw for senatorial sessions.

Senator Stanislaw Posner represented the Socialist Party in the Seym in 1922–1930, serving in 1928–1936 as deputy speaker of the senate. Senator Adam Czerniakow, member of the Pilsudski party in 1931–1935, was appointed during World War II by the Germans as the chairman of the Jewish Council (Judenrat) in the ghetto. Ordered by the Gestapo in July 1942 to sign an order of forced deportation of the Jews from the Warsaw ghetto to death camps, he committed suicide.

The Jewish Caucus in the Seym was headed by Isaac Grunbaum, a Zionist leader and a champion of Jewish immigration to Palestine. At a press conference in Warsaw on August 2, 1936, he said: "The market stall becomes gentrified in Poland. We have to leave. The time of the exodus of Jewish masses from Poland has come. Without emigration Poland would soon have five or six million Jews."

Many Poles of Jewish extraction were members of the government. The Ministry of Industry and Commerce was headed successively by Hipolit Gliwic, Czeslaw Klarner, and Henryk Floyar Reichman. The state Bank of Commerce was headed by Roman Gorecki, and the even larger financial institution, the Postal Savings Bank, by Henryk Gruber.

After Pilsudski's coup of 1926, there existed outside the formal government a "kitchen cabinet" called the "Colonels' Club." It included three colonels who had served in the Pilsudski Legion: Reichman, Wyzel-Sciezynski, and Librach.

Other former legionnaires, generals of Jewish origin, were Benedict Mond, army corps commander in Krakow, and Jacob Krzeminski, chairman of the State Board of Audit, one of the highest positions in the government.

The foreign office and the diplomatic service certainly did not discriminate against Jews. Franciszek Sokal was a member of the Polish delegation to the League of Nations in 1920–1924 and permanent delegate of Poland in 1926–1927. Thaddeus Gwiazdoski was head of the department at the foreign office, Wladyslaw Neuman ambassador to Norway, Karol Bader ambassador to nations of the Far East, Jan Ciechanowski the last Polish ambassador to the United States, Anatol Muhlstein counsellor at the Polish embassy in Paris, Emanuel Szerer legal counsel to the foreign office, Jan Weinstein deputy head of the consular department, Jan Fryling acting ambassador to India, and Jan Librach counsellor at the Paris embassy. In addition to these senior officials there were numerous foreign service officers of Jewish extraction.

While some Polish citizens of Jewish origin participated in the mainstream of political life, others formed their own Jewish political parties such as the socialist BUND, headed by Henryk Erlich, Victor Alter, and Leon Feiner, and the socialist workers' party Poalei Zion. These two parties differed in their view on emigration and conducted lively polemics. There was also the outlawed Polish Communist Party, whose leaders—Jacob Berman, Hilary Minc, Leon Chajn, Stefan Staszewski, and Eugene Szyr—played leading roles in 1945 and the following years.

The extensive participation of Jews in the political and cultural life of Poland and the willingness with which it was accepted by the Polish majority prove that the allegations of Polish anti-Semitism are ill founded. Eloquent testimony to that effect is offered by some members of the Jewish elite in Poland who survived the Holocaust and are now living in Israel. They are mostly natives of Krakow, and they dedicated to that "Polish Jerusalem" over a dozen books published in Israel. One example is the moving, witty, and emotional memoir of Rutterman-Abir,

Cracow Is Not Easy to Forget. The Ekked Publishing House in Tel
Aviv recently issued a volume entitled *Only the Legend Remains,*
which comprises ten items by eleven authors: Arthur Fischer,
Meir Bosak, Nathan Gross, Miriam Akavia, Halina Nelken, Feli-
cia Schechter-Karay, Irene Rothberg-Bronner, Joseph Bau,
Joseph Bosak, Miriam and Mordechai Peleg. They write about
Krakow's past and the Jewish presence in that city until the
Holocaust. They conjure memories of Krakow's beauty and
unique charm, of their lives in the "Jewish Jerusalem." There are
short stories, fragments of an intimate personal diary, essays
with lyrical overtones of longing for a paradise lost—a world of
youthful intellectual growth and opening horizons of the mind.
There are recollections of wise and good people, of close friend-
ships between Poles and Jews who shared their cultural values
and enriched each other. There are also accounts of the grim
years of the war and various responses to the tragedy, all in
flawless Polish. The publication was an initiative of the
Haubenstock Publishing Committee and the Cracovians' Circle
in Israel. They have already published ten books devoted to the
history of Krakow and its Jewish citizens.

That Polish-Jewish elite was quite unaware of the alleged basic
anti-Semitism of the Poles, as were the three million Jews who
had been living for centuries in close coexistence with Polish
peasants and workers. Neither of these classes had any anti-
Jewish tendencies. The peasants were accustomed to relying on
Jewish shopkeepers in small towns for all their purchases, while
the workers were influenced by the leading role played by the
Jews in the socialist party.

There was, however, an exception to that generally harmo-
nious coexistence. The National Democratic Party, founded by
Roman Dmowski, took a critical view of the role played in
Poland by the Jews. It claimed that the three million largely not
assimilated Jews, accounting for about 10 percent of the population, constituted an alien element detrimental to national unity.
It feared that the very high proportion of Jews in the professions
(estimated at 30 percent of the lawyers, doctors, architects, and

so forth), the Jewish monopoly in retail trade and finance, and the avoidance by the Jews of physical labor in mines, factories, or on the land amounted to barring the way of poorer Poles to social advancement. The National Democratic Party advocated as remedies the promotion of Polish small business and the boycott of Jewish stores. It also proposed quotas for the enroll-ment of university students so as to allow the admission of Gentile Poles, most of who could not afford the tuition fees. That policy, while directed against the Jews, was not inspired by any racial hatred of the Nazi type, but rather by economic com-petition between ethnic groups, a competition present in many countries. In any case, the National Democratic Party repre-sented less than 20 percent of the population. It advocated the emigration of the Jews from Poland to Palestine or other coun-tries; in this it had the support of the Jewish leadership.

The Polish government took the problem up officially at the League of Nations in Geneva.

The American writer Jerzy Kosinski commented on Polish-Jewish relations as follows:

> I am a writer, not a politician, my soul is Polish-Jewish, for it was formed by centuries of Jewish presence in Poland and in Polish culture, so that the two can never be separated. Only in Poland did a Jew have a chance of free spiritual growth, a fact which I always stress. Only there could the Jews build their own Jewish culture, while maintaining at the same time ties with the host nation. That is also the view of Abraham Heschel, a prominent theologian born in Poland, who wrote first in Polish and Yiddish, later in German and English. According to him the Jews found in Poland ideal conditions for psychological and philosophic development. "Any attempt to separate me from that millennium is unacceptable."
>
> The Polish host nation allowed us to find expression in our own spiritual language. No other nation would have permitted as much to a national and religious minority of such size, furthermore one in such contradiction with the New Testament. My parents and I were saved by Poles, I was hidden and transferred from one place to another and that with my looks! Polish readers don't know how I look, rather like the stereotype of a Jew in a Nazi poster. But let us not dwell on myself.

The Jews created in Poland a Jewish language, a Hassidic culture, their own messianism and philosophy, which made a contribution to the Jewish state through the intermediary of the Bund. That explains to some extent the reluctance of the Jews to reveal the past of their life in the diaspora, as it would have compelled them to admit their symbiosis with the Poles during the last thousand years.

CHAPTER III

Poland Under the German Occupation

THE SECOND WORLD WAR STARTED ON SEPTEMBER 1, 1939, WITH-
out any declaration of hostilities, when the Germans attacked Poland from three directions: from the west, from East
Prussia in the north, and from Slovakia in the south. To Poland's
rear was its border with the Soviet Union in the east.

The invading armies had overwhelming superiority over the
defenders. The invaders comprised seven armored divisions,
four motorized divisions, four light divisions, and three divisions of Slovak infantry—in all 1,800,000 men, 2,500 tanks, over
2,000 aircraft, and a naval squadron of warships.

The Polish defense force had twenty-four infantry divisions,
eight cavalry divisions, one armored-motorized division, five
mountain brigades, 166 tanks, and 236 aircraft, most of which
were destroyed on the ground in the first days of the war. When

fully mobilized, the Polish army would have counted 1,250,000, but mobilization was delayed under the influence of Poland's allies, France and Britain, who counseled moderation. Their mastery of the air and the speed of their armored and motorized units gave the Germans every advantage. Nevertheless, stubborn fighting continued an all fronts until September 17, when Poland was stabbed in the back by the Soviet invasion from the east. In spite of being surrounded on all sides, the Polish army went on fighting until October 5, inflicting heavy losses on the enemy and suffering even greater ones. During the "September campaign," Poland's allies in the West offered no assistance whatsoever, although they did declare war against Germany. Germany and the Soviet Union divided Poland, and the Poles immediately started organizing an underground resistance against both invaders.

Territories Incorporated into the Reich

Those who set about organizing the Polish underground had to face different conditions in each of the three zones into which Poland had been divided by the two invaders. In the western territories, incorporated into the Reich by Adolf Hitler's decree of October 8, 1939 (the districts of Poznan, Pomerania, Silesia, most of the Lodz district, the northern part of the Warsaw district, and smaller parts of the Krakow and Kielee districts), the Poles were stripped of all rights and subject, together with the Jews, to special legislation. To accommodate the influx of the new German population, arriving either from the Reich or from the USSR (through population exchange), Polish farms, workshops, medical and dental offices, business places, and houses were confiscated and turned over to the new settlers. Polish inhabitants of the territories incorporated into the Reich were transformed into serfs and forbidden under harsh penalties, like the serfs in olden days, to leave their places of work. In 1942, all Polish men born between 1910 and 1924 were registered on a *Volksliste* and forcibly drafted into the German army. A system of rationing that provided only bare sustenance (and of the worst quality), coupled with starvation wages, brought extreme hardships to the Polish population of these territories, particularly since all payments such as pensions or health insurance were stopped.

In addition, all secondary schools and institutions of higher learning were closed, while in the primary schools only the German language and arithmetic could be taught. The use of the Polish language outside of homes was forbidden; the Polish-language press was liquidated; libraries and bookshops were burned; archives and museums were either transferred to the Reich or destroyed; wayside chapels, roadside crosses, and tombstones in the cemeteries were demolished and the cemeteries themselves often plowed over; all Polish markers, inscriptions, and signboards were removed and the names of towns and villages changed to new German names. In essence, all traces of anything Polish were ruthlessly erased. Only one church was left in each county; all others were either burned down or closed. Sermons, prayers, and church hymns in Polish were forbidden. Most of the priests were arrested and sent to concentration camps.

Gradually, there began a forced transfer of population—particularly of the remnants of the intelligentsia—to the second German-occupied zone, the so-called *General Gouvernement*. This action affected two million people. They were permitted to take along only their personal effects. Loaded like cattle, they were transported in sealed cars to *General Gouvernement*, where they were dumped out, frequently at night, at a small railroad station or even in an open field.

Worst of all was the universal reign of terror and the stringent restrictions placed on individual freedom. Already in the very first days of the occupation, leaders in each community—particularly political leaders, mayors, landowners, local officials, priests, teachers, lawyers, and doctors—were seized and shot, executed publicly and ostentatiously in the market squares of their respective towns and villages. Those who escaped the early executions were to meet their end later in concentration camps or the prison at Mlynska Street in Poznan, where a guillotine had been installed and kept busy day and night. The town of Bydgoszcz was the most cruelly afflicted. In reprisal for the liquidation there of a German diversionary band by Polish military units at the very outset of the war (September 3–4, 1939), over twenty thousand inhabitants were murdered on the so-called "bloody Sunday."

A system evolved whereby every German, whether civilian or wearing the uniform of one of the innumerable military, party, auxiliary, or police organizations, became an absolute master over the life and death of any Pole. In practice this meant that any German could kill any Pole with impunity. There were many documented instances of murders because of some personal grudges dating back to prewar days, or because the victims were veterans of anti-German uprisings in Silesia or the Poznan district in 1918–1921. In addition, there were also sporadic killings. For instance, a Pole could, and often did, get shot for not getting off the sidewalk to make room for a German approaching from the opposite direction or for failing to take off his hat before a German. People were also killed for illicit fishing, for slaughtering a pig for their own use, for stealing fruit from the orchards, for riding a train without a ticket. German courts pronounced wholesale death sentences, primarily for so-called "economic sabotage" and for infractions against even the least important regulations imposed by the invaders, which ordinarily and under normal conditions would bring no more than an arrest and a fine.

One particularly shocking case was that of Zofia Czechon, a Polish woman sentenced by the court in Plock to a fine of one thousand German marks or three months in jail because her dog, although muzzled, had the effrontery to "bark hostilely and snarl" at the dog of the German *Oberinspektor* Richard Kunat.

As far as restrictions on individual freedom were concerned, the ban on free movement, particularly on travel by railroad, was the most keenly felt. In order to travel anywhere, one had to obtain a pass, stating in detail the route to be taken and the

duration of the trip. All bicycles owned by Poles were confiscated. The only exception was made for those who worked far
away from their homes; but in those instances, their passes
prescribed precisely the route they were to take to their places of
work. To veer from this route meant to incur severe punishment, in addition to beating, kicking, and face-slapping.

All Germans—both those who had lived on those territories
before the war and those who later swarmed over the territories
incorporated into the Reich—were expected to spy on their
Polish neighbors, not only at their places of work, but also
generally elsewhere, and had to report everything they observed to the authorities. In one word, the territories incorporated into the Reich were turned into one big prison ruled by the
dreaded Gestapo.

Everything was done with one goal in mind—to change those
lands over into truly German lands and to get rid of those Poles
who could not be exterminated by transferring them to the
General Gouvernement.

Despite this reign of terror and the strict restrictions placed
on individual freedom, the underground movement in the western territories sprang into existence spontaneously, as it did in
all Poland. The cities of Poznan and Lodz were the leaders. In
order to appreciate what was involved, one has to understand
the "facts of life" of the conspiracy. A conspiracy is impossible
without a regular contact between its members, either in one
locality or in several places, often far apart. Thus it was necessary to travel a great deal and to stay overnight or meet people in
various places without registering with the police (as required)
and without attracting the attention of German neighbors. It was
also necessary to transport letters, underground publications,
and arms. Finally, conspiratorial activities required a certain
mobility within the immediate neighborhood. All this was out of
the question in the incorporated territories, and yet the underground network came into being because the brave people of
Silesia, Pomerania, and the district of Poznan knew how to
circumvent innumerable orders and prohibitions and how to
overcome all obstacles at the risk of life and freedom. Though

the underground network in the western territories was handicapped, as compared with the organization built under considerably easier conditions prevailing in the *General Gouvernement*, still it managed to extend its operations even over the prewar frontier of the Reich, as far as the Opole Silesia.

Territories Incorporated into the USSR

Under the Soviet occupation—which included the districts of Wilno, Polesie, Bialystok, Wolyn, Tarnopol, Lwow, and Stanislawow—conditions were much the same. Although these districts were also incorporated, the procedure which made them a part of the USSR was far more refined than that adopted by the Germans. Instead of the brutal Nazi decree of incorporation, elections were ordered to be held on October 22, 1939. On that day, the inhabitants of those territories, terrorized by the NKVD, "elected" 2,410 delegates, handpicked by the NKVD and drawn for the most part from among the newly arrived Russians, totally unknown to the local people. Thus elected, the delegates then applied to the Supreme Council in Moscow for the admission of the "liberated" eastern Polish territories into the Soviet Union. The Supreme Soviet graciously granted their request, and by the decrees of November 1 and November 2, 1939, the northern districts were incorporated into the Byelorussian SSR and the southern districts into the Ukrainian SSR. The final result was the same as in the west, but the method of incorporation permitted the Soviets to parry all accusations of force and violence by claiming the "spontaneous will of the people." A crowning touch was added to this lawless procedure with the decree of November 29, 1939, which conferred Soviet citizenship on all inhabitants of the occupied territories; in consequence, all young men were made subject to military service in the Soviet army.

A succession of "economic reforms" accomplished results that were identical with those achieved by the Nazi policies in the west—the Polish population was reduced to utter destitution.

The Soviets took over not only all prewar Polish state property, but also all private estates, factories, sugar refineries, distilleries, saw mills, and all other industrial enterprises, banks, and savings institutions. They then proceeded to loot this wealth by carrying it away to the USSR. Many factories were closed, creating unemployment. The Polish currency *(zloty)* was taken out of circulation, and all bank and savings accounts were blocked. Ruthless requisitions by the Soviet army of both food and feed, as well as frantic buying out of store inventories by the imported Soviet military and civilian employees, created such shortages that even salt and matches became unavailable, and poverty reigned supreme.

In the eastern territories, too, all traces of a Polish past were doomed to obliteration. Instead of the Polish language, the Ukrainian and the Byelorussian were introduced as official languages. This decree was on paper only, for in practice this meant the Russian language. Thousands of churches, monasteries, and convents were closed and their buildings put to other uses. Roadside chapels were torn down, here as in the west, and roadside crosses were hacked down and burned.

The greatest similarities between the two oppressors, however, could be found in their deportation policies. From the western territories, the Germans forcibly deported about two million people to the *General Gouvernement*. From the eastern territories, the Russians—in four massive operations—deported into the depths of the Soviet Union, mostly to Asia, about 1,700,000 people. Both the German and the Soviet operations were carried out with one goal in mind—to strip the occupied territories of all Polish elements. Both were conducted with the same utter ruthlessness. Men, women, and children were snatched from their homes without any warning and permitted to take with them only the barest personal necessities.

Only in the field of education did the two invaders' policies show any marked variations. The Germans closed all secondary schools and all institutions of higher learning, while in the primary schools only German and arithmetic were permitted to be taught. The Russians, on the other hand, retained the prewar structure of the educational system, but converted all programs along Soviet patterns and introduced variations based on nationality. Study of the Russian language was compulsory, as was history (Soviet brand) and subjects required in Soviet schools, such as political-ideological indoctrination. All schools were divided into Ukrainian, Byelorussian, Jewish, and Polish. In this last group, the Polish language was tolerated. The aim of such a system of education, reinforced by a flood of propaganda through radio and films, was to indoctrinate according to Communist lights the youth of all four national groups.

The policy of terror was instituted immediately after Poland's eastern territories were occupied by the Soviet armies. Hundreds of priests and monks, judges, prosecutors, police officers, political and social leaders, deputies and senators, government functionaries, and officials of local governments were murdered outright. The slaughter reached its peak after the outbreak of the Nazi-Soviet war on June 21, 1941, when all political prisoners were murdered. Total Polish losses due to this policy of murder are estimated at close to 100,000 people. Included in this number are 15,000 army officers (mostly from the reserves, i.e., men who in civilian life formed the backbone of the educated and professional classes in Poland) who were interned in the USSR after September 17, 1939, and murdered in the spring of 1940. The mass grave of some of these officers was found by the Germans in 1941 in the Katyn Forest near Smolensk. It contained 4,253 bodies.

Although the two occupiers used different methods of control in many respects, the final result was always the same. The Germans exercised a highly visible, almost physical control over nearly every move of every Pole. The Soviets tolerated free moving about while exercising equally strict control in a less obvious way, mostly with the help of the local Communists, familiar with the local scene, as well as large numbers of recruited local informers. In the western territories, national differences formed an abyss between the oppressors and the oppressed, and made it more difficult for the Germans to establish control. In the eastern territories, however, the surveillance was facilitated by the fact that, with the exception of the NKVD, both those who exercised control and those who were controlled belonged to one of the four national groups—Polish, Ukrainian, Byelorussian, or Jewish. Finally, in building up a network of surveillance, the NKVD cunningly took advantage of various national antagonisms, playing up the so-called national minorities against the Poles. This scheme created a double crisscrossing, and therefore a more efficient network of control.

Even so, the rise of the underground movement could not be stemmed. In the eastern territories, as in all Poland, it came into being spontaneously, particularly in the cities and towns where the Polish population was in a majority, even in those areas where the villages in the surrounding countryside were predominantly Byelorussian or Ukrainian. The cities of Lwow and Wilno were the leaders. Even though the conditions under which the underground movement in Soviet-occupied Poland was born were somewhat easier than in the territories incorporated into the Reich, it was still impossible for the movement to develop as well as in the *General Gouvernement*. The situation changed radically, and for the better, only after the outbreak of the Nazi-Soviet war on June 21, 1941, and after the lightning takeover of these territories by the Germans. Although the line of demarcation between the *General Gouvernement* and the former Soviet-occupied zone was maintained, which made all communication difficult, still the underground in the eastern territories from that time on became very similar to the underground in the *General Gouvernement*, if for no other reason than the selfsame identity and methods of the oppressor.

The General Gouvernement (GG)

Hitler's decree of October 12, 1939, created the so-called *General Gouvernement*, with a population of about twelve million people. It was carved out of the Lublin district, part of the Lwow district, and most of the Warsaw, Krakow, and Kielce districts. The *General Gouvernement* was designated, in the first stage of the German master plan, as a gathering place for all Poles. They were to become a nation of serfs, a reservoir of labor, doomed to extinction during the later stages of the plan, either through a massive German colonization or through various measures aimed at biological destruction (e.g., a ban on marriages, hunger, overwork), or finally—and assuming, of course, Germany's ultimate victory over the Soviet Union—through deportation of all the surviving Poles to Siberia (General Eastern Plan). Only the Jews were to fare worse than the Poles, according to the plan. They were to be confined in ghettos within the *General Gouvernement* and killed off in concentration camps during the first stage of the plan.

The initial attack—both in the territories incorporated into the Reich and those incorporated into the USSR—was directed against the intelligentsia, the so-called leading class, marked for destruction. Individual arrests were conducted on a massive scale. Political and social leaders, deputies and senators, professors and scholars, judges, attorneys, doctors, industrialists, government officials, reserve officers were swept into the net. Those taken in Warsaw were first placed in the Pawiak prison and later taken to concentration camps in Germany. When the Auschwitz concentration camp was opened on June 14, 1940, most of them were sent there. Large-scale operations against the intelligentsia began with the arrest of 115 professors of the Krakow University on November 6, 1939; they were taken to the Sachsenhausen concentration camp, where many of them perished. The first mass execution took place in Wawer near Warsaw on December 27, 1939. On that day, 107 men were snatched from their homes in the middle of the night and shot summarily in reprisal for the wounding of two German soldiers by a Polish criminal. Beginning with June 20, 1940, mass executions were carried out in the Palmiry Woods, which became a sort of handy execution place where the people of Warsaw were taken to be shot. The first street roundup took place in Warsaw on May 8, 1940; over a thousand people were seized on that day and carried off to concentration camps in Germany, many of them never to return. Similar street roundups were also staged in other cities of the *General Gouvernement*. Finally, on November 25, 1940, the Warsaw ghetto was sealed off from the world, shutting within its walls over half a million Jews condemned to a death of starvation or—those who managed to survive—in gas chambers of the concentration camps in Treblinka, Chelm, Auschwitz, and others. Successive waves of terror rolled on one after another, designed gradually to destroy the population of the recalcitrant cities, particularly the intelligentsia, and to terrorize all Poles into docile subservience to the will of the oppressor.

The high point of terror—aside from the unprecedented in the history of mankind extermination of some six million Jews, both Polish and those brought to Poland from other countries— were the mass executions staged on the streets of cities, towns, and villages of the *General Gouvernement*. The slaughter was conducted ostensibly in order to carry out a decree issued by Governor Hans Frank on October 2, 1943, aimed at the suppression of all attempts to thwart the German work of reconstruction in the *General Gouvernement*. This decree prescribed the death penalty for infractions of even the most insignificant German regulations, let alone decrees and orders. The death penalty could be meted out, for instance, for illegal slaughter or sale of meat, for raising prices, and other similar offenses. Under the guise of this decree, in Warsaw alone, between October 15, 1943, and August 1, 1944, when the Warsaw Rising broke out, about 9,500 people were caught in the streets and shot, often in the very heart of the city (3,213 according to the official German statistics). After the prisoners' work details removed the bodies from the place of execution, people of Warsaw would cover the site with flowers, light candles, and kneel down in prayer. Not infrequently, the kneeling mourners were shot, too. As for the rest of the country, detailed statistics are not available, but the losses are estimated at several thousand. The goal of these executions, amounting to the murder of individuals picked at random, was always the same—to terrorize the rebellious Poles and to cow them into total submission.

Simultaneously, there began a wholesale exploitation of the

country, which was to provide labor and food for the Reich. Huge delivery quotas of grain, cattle, butter, milk, and eggs were imposed, stripping the countryside of all food. Only universally practiced sabotage (punishable by death) made it possible for people in the countryside to survive and even to smuggle some food to the cities, whose inhabitants received only subsistence rations, too small to live on but too large to die of starvation. Everybody was compelled to work. Throughout the occupation years, some two million people were shipped off to the Reich for forced labor.

All secondary and higher educational institutions in GG were closed; the teaching of history and geography in primary and trade schools was prohibited. All museums, archives, and libraries were liquidated and their contents either destroyed or taken to Germany. Historical monuments and markers were destroyed, as was everything that could remind people of Poland's history. Finally, all state industries became the property of the Reich, while private enterprises, larger farms, and estates were turned over to German trustees, which was tantamount to expropriation.

Still, there were considerable differences between conditions prevailing in the territories incorporated into the Reich or into the Soviet Union and those in the *General Gouvernement*. The most important of these was that the population of the *General Gouvernement* was not subject to forced resettlement, while in other parts of Poland whole families were uprooted from their native regions and transferred to regions that were foreign to them both nationally and geographically, such as the Asiatic parts of Russia, where they were doomed to perish. Even in a more congenial area of resettlement, such as the *General Gouvernement*, transferred multitudes had no chance of leading a normal life, but had to subsist with the help of relatives, chance acquaintances, or charitable organizations. Deportations to the Reich for forced labor differed from mass deportations in that they affected only individuals and did not uproot entire families: The only mass population transfer carried out by the Germans took place in the Zamosc region, where 110,000 peasants from 297 communities were uprooted in order to make room for the German colonists. However, violent military counteraction by the underground, burning down of the villages where the new German settlers were installed, and, finally, the setbacks suffered by the German armies on the eastern front combined to make the Germans abandon this operation.

The *General Gouvernement* also differed from territories incorporated into the Reich in that the Polish language was retained there, as were the Polish state and local governmental institutions, such as lower courts, fiscal machinery, police, and the city and county administrations. The Polish Red Cross was permitted to function and so was a charitable organization called the Central Welfare Council. The Bank of Poland also was permitted to operate, though under a changed name, and was used by the Germans to introduce a separate currency for the *General Gouvernement*. Also permitted to function was the National Economic Bank and the Postal Savings Bank. The scope of activities of the Association of Cooperatives, *Spolem*, was extended to warehouse the levied food delivery quotas and to distribute among the population the scant supplies available to the Poles.

All legitimate theaters were closed, but small theaters were allowed to open with new programs, mostly pornographic, forced on them by the German propaganda. All Polish publications were banned except for the so-called "reptile press," subservient to the Germans, whose existence, however—since it appeared in Polish—served to emphasize the difference between the *General Gouvernement* and the terrorities incorporated into the Reich.

Finally, in GG much more freedom was allowed in moving from place to place and also within the confines of one's immediate neighborhood, even though a curfew was enforced. No restrictions on travel, such as those in the incorporated territories, were imposed. Control of documents, search of luggage, and arrest if anything prohibited was found, represented the only threat to those traveling by railroad. This made it possible, even though risky, to smuggle food supplies without which no larger city in Poland could have survived the years of German occupation.

The leniency of these restrictions—as compared with the hellish conditions under which Poles were forced to live in the incorporated territories—was in keeping with the provisions of "stage one" of the German plan for Poland, according to which conditions in the *General Gouvernement* were to be maintained at a level supporting a primitive existence for several millions of Polish robots. In order, however, to impress the Poles with the utter futility of all national aspirations, the Germans built up in *GG* a huge apparatus of terror similar to that operating in the incorporated territories and dealing out the death penalty or imprisonment in concentration camps for even the most petty offenses. Of all the German-occupied countries, that part of Poland that was known as the *General Gouvernement* had the greatest concentration of the Gestapo, headed by individuals handpicked for their ruthlessness. A network of thousands of informers, recruited from among the riffraff and from the *Volksdutsche* (i.e., Polish citizens of German ancestry, listed on special registers) was established. The Gestapo were also assisted by units of gendarmerie and by such police formations as the *Grenzschutz* (border guard), the *Bahnschutz* (railroad police), the *Werkschutz* (factory guard), and others. Every German and every *Volksdeutsch* had to belong to the *Selbschutz* (self-defense organization), which was also utilized against the Polish population of *GG*. In addition, German military intelligence and criminal police were also brought into play, while the Polish police were limited to keeping general order. The German control over the Polish populations was further strengthened by additional SS units composed of volunteers from among the Ukrainians, Latvians, Estonians, Lithuanians, and—during the last period of the occupation—also Russians, the so-called Vlasovites.

The terror apparatus described above operated in every city and every town in the *General Gouvernement*. To subjugate the countryside to the same extent proved impracticable, for it would have required hundreds of thousands of military and police personnel. Nonetheless, the countryside, too, was under the strict surveillance of gendarmerie units, stationed in smaller towns and villages. German punitive and repressive measures were even more severe in the country than in the cities, because they involved wholesale destruction of entire villages by murder and fire.

The Pattern of Struggle

Every inhabitant of the *General Gouvernement* lived in constant awareness of the huge structure of terror. He woke up fully alerted to it; he could sense it throughout the day in the streets, in workplaces, in cafés, even in churches. He went to sleep continuously conscious of its existence, and bolted out of his bed, instantly awake, at the slightest sound in the street, in the house entrance, or on the stairway. Even if the night went peacefully by, he could never be sure on leaving his house in the morning whether he would return there at night. At any moment he could be caught in a street roundup, or he could inadvertently enter a place where a trap had been set for all comers. When going away for any length of time, people always said their last good-byes and bid their families farewell as if they were going off to wars; often they did not come back and were never heard from again.

Members of the underground movement, which flourished in the more lenient climate of the *General Gouvernement*, faced a double danger. In addition to random mass arrests, they were also threatened by planned actions directed against particular individuals, since the Gestapo pursued the underground men with rabid doggedness. Death was the constant companion of every member of the underground. At night in the room where he hid a false identity or without registering, he risked a Gestapo night raid, if they were looking for him. During the day, when he went out on the streets, he had to make his way past the Gestapo agents, provided with his description or photograph. Every appointment, every meeting, every delivery of messages, radio bulletins, or copies of the underground press, let alone things such as a clandestine military briefing, troop exercises, work in an underground editorial office, printing shop, broadcasting station, or gun shop—generally speaking, any activity connected with the underground—required courage, alertness, utmost caution, great presence of mind, cunning and—of most importance—luck. Without these there was an ever-present threat of arrest, torture, and, frequently, death.

The Gestapo hierarchy were doubtless familiar with the history of Poland, for they had foreseen far in advance that an underground organization would come into being in Poland. In a series of secret German-Soviet agreements, concluded both before and after the German invasion of Poland, there was also an agreement pertaining to mutual assistance in combating the Polish resistance movement. According to the terms of this agreement, the Gestapo and the NKVD were to share all information that could be helpful to either of them in suppressing the underground. The Gestapo moved against the underground with typical German thoroughness. An effort was made, with the help of a broad network of agents, to penetrate and infiltrate the underground. In a constant search for clues, a thorough study of the underground press was carried on; underground couriers, contact girls, and "mail drops" were ferreted out; broadcasting stations were tracked down and their output monitored and decoded. Constant search went on for underground printing plants, munitions workshops, and secret meeting places. Various underground groups and their leaders were assigned to particular Gestapo men, each of who concentrated exclusively on a given individual or group.

The underground fought back by means of counterintelligence, coups directed against the more prominent Gestapo men, attacks on local gendarmerie posts, assassinations of Gestapo agents, disguises, and masterly forgeries of documents such as the obligatory *kennkarten* (identity cards), birth certificates, work certificates, registration cards, various permits and passes issued by the Germans, and many other legalizing documents. Meeting places, living quarters, and overnight shelters were camouflaged and constantly shifted; varied passwords and warning signals were devised; hiding places and caches were constructed and secreted in most unlikely places; personal contacts were limited to a minimum, as was the use of any written communications or memoranda; meeting places, printing shops, and broadcasting installations were assured of a measure of security by dint of constant surveillance and frequently also by posting an armed guard. But the cardinal weapon of the resistance was silence. To keep silent and to guard the secret was the first and the most important commandment of conspiracy, and it was always included in the underground oath. Hundreds paid dearly for their fidelity to this oath, dying in torture or taking their own lives rather than betray secrets of the underground. (Total losses in human lives in Poland during World War II are estimated at 6 million; of this number 3.5 million were Polish citizens of Jewish faith.)

It was against such a background and in the midst of such a struggle that the Polish underground movement was born to wage a war whose toll was to be counted in thousands. Against all odds, it grew stronger and stronger from month to month and from year to year, until it finally evolved at its highest point into the Polish Underground State, which had its own government, administration, parliament, jurisdiction, army, education, welfare, press—in sum, all the institutions and attributes of an independent state. It came to be recognized throughout the world as the leading underground movement of World War II, and Poland was hailed as an "inspiration to the free world."

The highest recognition, however, was to come from the enemy himself. On the eve of Germany's final defeat, the question of organizing an underground resistance movement in Germany came up for consideration. Various options were reviewed, and the Polish model of underground organization was chosen as the best to adopt.

CHAPTER IV

The Jews Under the Occupation

THE LOT OF POLISH CITIZENS OF JEWISH ORIGIN WHO FOUND themselves in areas occupied by the Soviets after the outbreak of World War II appeared to be tied to that of the country of their birth. With the outbreak of the Soviet-German war in 1941 and after Stalin signed an agreement with the Polish premier in exile, General Sikorski, four thousand Jews, among whom was Menachem Begin, found themselves in the ranks of a Polish army which was being formed within the USSR under the leadership of General Wladyslaw Anders. This army, after being evacuated from the Soviet Union, marched through Iran arriving in Palestine in 1942, where all of the Jewish soldiers were faced with a crucial decision as to whether they should remain in Palestine or stay with the Anders army to fight in Italy against the Nazis. General Anders aided these soldiers in reaching a decision when he issued a confidential instruction that Polish-Jewish soldiers who wished to remain in Palestine would not be looked upon as deserters. Approximately three thousand soldiers decided to stay; about one thousand remained in the ranks of the II Polish Army Corps, which fought in the Italian campaign. In the military cemetery at Monte Cassino in Italy, the author personally counted eighteen graves bearing the Star of David. (He did not have occasion to visit two similar Polish Army cemeteries near Bologna and Ancona.)

Polish army Corporal Menachem Begin chose a third path. In deciding whether he should remain in Palestine or fight the Nazis he stated: "The army whose uniform I wear and to which I swore allegiance fights with the mortal enemy of the Jewish nation, the Nazi Germany. One cannot desert from such an army even to fight for the freedom of one's own fatherland."

Begin would have remained with the Polish army if it had not been for a happy accident. The deputy commander of the Anders II Army Corps was General Michal Tokarzewski, a member of Pilsudski legions and an organizer of the Polish anti-Hitler underground in 1939 who, while crossing the border from German-occupied Poland to Soviet-occupied Poland in 1940, was arrested by the Soviet NKVD, only to be subsequently released like Begin from the Soviet concentration camp after the outbreak of the Soviet-German war in 1941.

The fortunes of war also drove to Palestine Wiktor Tomir Drymmer, the former director of the department in the Polish Ministry of Foreign Affairs who handled aid to Irgun and Hagana, Zionist fighting organizations. He immediately established secret contact with Irgun which, as the owner of a print shop, began to publish the *Independent Bulletin* for the members of the Anders army. In addition, Irgun gave the Polish military authorities a friendly suggestion that if they identified their military vehicles with Polish emblems they would not be subjected to Irgun attacks which were directed against the British.

At the request of Irgun, Drymmer approached his colleague from the Anders army, General Tokarzewski, and asked him to release Menachem Begin from active duty because he was needed by the Jewish organization. As a former underground leader who not only had complete understanding of the activities which were being conducted, and because he was sympathetic to the objectives of the Jewish underground, the General gave Begin unlimited furlough.

There was nothing which could now stand in Menachem Begin's way to become the leader of the Irgun Zvai Leumi, the first step on the road which led to his assumption of the premiership of an independent Jewish state for which he fought all of his life.

Itzhak Shamir (Jeziernicki) did not have the problems which faced Begin in being released from the Polish army even though he did escape British pursuit dressed in a Polish noncommissioned officer's uniform while using genuine military credentials which he surreptitiously obtained, and by pretending that he spoke only Polish. Since he was not a member of the Polish armed forces, when the need for concealment passed he simply donned civilian clothes.

Organizing a Holocaust

At the outbreak of the war, there were 3.5 million Jews in Poland—about 10 percent of the total population. This high percentage was the result of a long historical process. In 1264, Prince Boleslas the Pious of Kalisz granted the Jews a statute guaranteeing their religious freedom and autonomy for Jewish communities. When persecutions of Jews broke out in other European countries, there began a mass migration of Jews to Poland, where subsequent centuries of tolerance favored the growth of the Jewish population and the establishment of centers of Jewish culture in cities such as Lublin and Wilno.

Following Poland's partition into occupation zones in 1939, about two million Jews remained in the *General Gouvernement* and in the western territories incorporated into the Reich, while the rest were in the Soviet-occupied zone. When the war broke out between Russia and Germany, with the lightning German occupation of all Polish territories, another million Polish Jews fell under German rule. The rest (about half a million) had been deported previously, together with the Poles, into the depths of Russia. Some Jews also managed to make their way to the Scandinavian countries (through Lithuania, before that country was overrun by the Soviets) and the West, or they obtained Japanese visas and, crossing the USSR in transit, reached Japan and went on to, for instance, Australia.

German policy regarding the Polish Jews was formulated in the decree of the Central Security Office of the Reich of September 21, 1939, pertaining to the solution of the Jewish problem by stages. The final goal of complete extermination of the Jews was not spelled out in the decree and remained a state secret. The decree specified, among others, concentrations of Jews in larger cities, in designated districts. The Security Office was headed by Reinhard Heydrich, and it was on his behalf that Adolf Eichmann undertook the implementation of the decree.

To begin with, the Jews were ordered to wear armbands with the Star of David; this was followed by confiscation of all Jewish real estate and partial confiscation of private property. Jews were ousted from all public institutions, but—through a decree of Governor Hans Frank of October 26, 1939—were subject to compulsory labor from the age of sixteen to sixty. In this connection, special labor camps were established (at the peak of this action, there were three hundred such camps). Finally, on January 26, 1940, the Jews were forbidden to move from one place to another and to use public means of transportation.

However, the most shattering blow came with the establishment of closed ghettos to which Jews from the entire country were driven, though there were also instances of on-the-spot extermination of Jews in small localities, for example, in Kleczew (Konin county). In Warsaw, the ghetto was established in November 1940; in Lodz, already at the beginning of 1940; in Krakow, only in March 1941. Governor Frank's decree of October 25, 1941, stated that:

"Jews who leave their designated districts are subject to the penalty of death. The same penalty will be applied to persons who knowingly provide shelter for such Jews"—that is, to Poles.

The same regulation was reiterated time and again in many decrees issued by local German authorities throughout the years of occupation. The death penalty also threatened the Jews for illegal purchase of food, for using public transportation, for not wearing the prescribed armband. For that matter, the killing of a Jew by a German for whatever reason, or for no reason at all, was not punishable since Jews and gypsies were removed from the protection of the law by the decree of March 4, 1941.

According to the letter of the decree, any person with three grandparents who had been members of a Jewish religious community was Jewish. As a result, there were many people in the ghettos whose parents had already changed their religious affiliation, and who did not consider themselves Jews at all.

Both in the labor camps and in the ghettos, the Jewish population was doomed to a slow death by starvation, exhaustion, and illness. The daily food ration in the Warsaw ghetto was the equivalent of 184 calories. In consequence, the mortality rate—particularly among children and older people—was extremely high, several times higher than before the war. One contributing factor was the unbelievable concentration of population, with a dozen people or more living in one room.

Among the thousands of the inmates of what became the largest prison in the world, a ghetto circled by walls and guards, a continuous debate on how to save one's life continued day and night. People analyzed the two thousand years of life in the Diaspora, the religious persecutions, the Russian pogroms, their assimilation in other countries. They studied assiduously the Talmud, the Bible, the Old Testament, rabbinical writings, and various holy books. There were confrontations between Orthodoxy and more moderate forms of Judaism, between socialist and nationalist movements, each seeking a political solution. The consensus which emerged was unanimous in the belief that only total submission to all the Nazi orders and industrious work for the Germans might offer chances of survival until the end of the war. One should abstain from any anti-German activity, rule out anything like the guerrilla campaign waged by the Polish underground just outside the walls of the ghetto, forget about the Polish army fighting in the west against the Reich. The watchword was: "This is not our war; it's the war of the Poles against the Germans." All the Jewish problems were to be dealt with by the Jewish Council (Judenrat), headed by the former Polish senator Adam Czerniakow and formed by the Germans themselves. That doctrine of submissiveness remained in force for over two years, during which the Jews in the ghetto did not ask the Poles for any help or weapons. Only the smuggling of food to the ghetto flourished; this was tolerated by the Germans. It was the subject of Jack Eisner's book *The Survivor.*

Disenchantment and a basic turnaround did not come until the third year of the war, when in July of 1942 the last stage was reached—extermination of all the Jews gathered behind the walls of the *General Gouvernement* ghettos. It began with mass executions of Jews in eastern Poland and in Russia by the so-called *Einsatzgruppen*, which moved in after the outbreak of the German-Soviet war, following on the heels of swiftly advancing German armies. In the spring of 1942, the Germans began transports of the ghetto populations to the extermination camps of Auschwitz, Treblinka, Majdanek, Sobibor, Belzec, and Chelm (this last one, for Jews from the territories incorporated into the Reich), as well as a few other, smaller ones. Once in camp, the Jews were killed in the gas chambers and their corpses cremated or stacked outside in big piles and burned. The first transports from the Warsaw ghetto to Treblinka began on July 22, 1942. Within two months, 300,000 Jews (out of the total ghetto population of 400,000) were evacuated from the Warsaw ghetto.

Hundreds of thousands of Jews brought from Italy, Germany, France, Belgium, Holland, Austria, and Czechoslovakia were murdered in German death camps in Poland. According to the calculations of the Institute of Jewish Affairs in New York, of a total of 9,612,000 Jews in Europe, 5,787,000 perished under German occupation; of this number, 1,500,000 were killed in the countries of their residence, primarily in German-occupied parts of the USSR.

Jewish sources estimate the number of Polish Jews that were saved from the Holocaust at between 50,000 and 120,000. According to the estimates of the Directorate of Civil Resistance, there were about 200,000 Jewish survivors in Poland.

Marek Edelman, still living, a hero of the Warsaw ghetto uprising, estimated the number of Jews in hiding in Warsaw at 18,000 and that of the Poles sheltering them at 100,000, assuming that about five persons were required to protect one Jew over a period of time. That estimate seems to be understated, because the hiding of one person over a period of four to five years required changing the site every few months and consequently would mean the involvement of at least ten families, each comprising several members. Every member of a family hiding Jews risked summary execution. Therefore the total number of Varsovians who risked their lives to save Jews must have been much larger than 100,000.

The two thousand Yad Vashem medals awarded by Israel to Poles who helped Jews during the occupation seem a meager recognition of the many thousands who risked their lives to save those of their Jewish wards.

Liaison with the Ghetto

The underground leadership, and particularly the Government Delegate in London and the Home Army (which included a few Jewish officers in its High Command), began to publish daily in their underground press information about the persecutions of Jews, which they denounced in the strongest terms, calling on the Polish population to render the Jews all possible assistance. *Biuletyn Informacyjny*, organ of the Home Army, even had its own correspondent in the ghetto (Jerzy Grasberg). Similarly, Polish underground political parties established contact with their members or counterpart organizations behind the ghetto walls. Thus, members of the Jewish BUND maintained regular contact with the Polish Socialist Party (WRN), and the Polish Boy Scouts (the Grey Ranks) were in touch with the Jewish *Hashomer Hacair*. The same was also true for the Democratic Party. Among the smaller underground organizations maintaining either contacts or affiliated cells in the ghetto, were the Security Corps (responsible for saving about five thousand Jews during the war), a leftist organization called "Spartakus," a youth organization called "Union of Struggle for Liberation," and the organization of Polish Socialists, which had its chapter in the ghetto. When the Polish Workers Party came into existence in January 1942, it also established a cell in the Warsaw ghetto.

As early as in 1940, the Government Delegate alerted London about the persecution of Jews in Poland. Thereupon, the Polish government-in-exile sent a note on this subject to Allied governments (May 3, 1941). Also in 1941, the Polish Ministry of Information in London published a booklet on the persecution of Jews in Poland. It was entitled *Bestiality Unknown in Any Previous Record of History* and was based on information received from occupied Poland. In January 1942, the Ministry issued another publication, *The New German Order in Poland*. Both publications created a stir throughout the Allied world, which after 1941 could no longer plead ignorance of the persecution of Jews in Poland.

The Jewish Underground

About that time, the first preparations for armed resistance began in the ghettos. In October 1942, leaders of the incipient Jewish underground joined in forming the Jewish National Committee, composed of representatives of all Jewish organizations, with the exception of BUND. This led to the creation of the Coordination Commission, which logically became in time the central political body of the Jewish underground. Irrespective of this, both BUND and the Jewish National Committee had their separate representatives remaining "on the Aryan side" and maintaining regular contact with the Government Delegate. Dr. Adolf Berman (Borowski) represented the Jewish National Committee, and Dr. Leon Feiner (Berezowski) was the representative of BUND.

On July 28, 1942, the Fighting Organization of the Warsaw ghetto was born. "On the Aryan side," it was represented by Arie Wilner (pseudonym: Jurek). On December 2, 1942, the Fighting Organization, its composition enlarged by that time, took a new name: Jewish Fighting Organization (*Zydowska Organizacja Bojowa*—ZOB). The Jewish Fighting Organization was commanded by Mordecai Anielewicz. At the time of the Ghetto Uprising, it had about twenty-two combat groups (between twenty and thirty men in each), over seven hundred combat soldiers in all. Liaison with the Home Army was maintained by Arie Wilner, who was in touch with the head of the Jewish section of the High Command of the Home Army, Henryk Wolinski (pseudonym: Waclaw).

The Jewish representatives—Adolf Berman for the Jewish National Committee, Leon Feiner for BUND, and Arie Wilner for the Jewish Fighting Organization—declared their willingness to subordinate the activities of their organizations to the Government Delegate and the High Command of the Home Army. At the same time they asked for arms and ammunition, financial assistance, and help with the training. The Delegate accepted the declaration and promised to extend help, while the commander of the Home Army, in his order of November 11, 1942, acknowledged the Jewish Fighting Organization as a paramilitary organization and instructed them to employ the Home Army's organizational methods and fighting tactics. Simultaneously, the High Command assigned Major Stanislaw Weber (pseudonym: Chirurg) and Captain Zbigniew Lewandowski (pseudonym: Szyna) to organize assistance for the Jewish Fighting Organization. Accordingly, the first ten guns and ammunition were passed on to the Jewish Fighting Organization in December 1942, and another ten guns and ammunition in January 1943. For his part, the Government Delegate established the

Jewish section of his office, headed at first by Witold Bienkowski (pseudonym: Kalski) and later by Wladyslaw Bartoszewski (pseudonym: Ludwik), who was decorated after the war with the Israeli medal of Yad Vashem.

Thus the historic joining together of the Polish and the Jewish underground movements was completed. The manner in which it was accomplished testified to the loyalty of the Jewish citizens of Poland to the Polish state.

Also active in the ghetto was another Jewish military organization, which did not merge with the Jewish Fighting Organization. The Jewish Military Union (*Zydowki Zwiazek Wojskowy*—ZZW) consisted of three combat groups, about four hundred men in all, mostly former officers and noncommissioned officers of the Polish army and members of a Zionist organization, BETAR. It was commanded by Pawel Frenkel. The Jewish Military Union established contact with the Government Delegate and the High Command of the Home Army through a Polish underground organization, the Security Corps.

Within the framework of cooperation between the Polish and the Jewish underground, and at the request of Leon Feiner, the High Command of the Home Army sent a dispatch to Jewish organizations in London, which responded by forwarding through the Home Army channels the first $5,000 for BUND. This initiated other, more frequent and larger shipments of money sent to the Jewish organizations via the underground channels of the Government Delegate and the High Command of the Home Army. Contact was also established, by means of the Home Army and the Delegate's transmitters, with Jewish organizations in the United States.

The Council of Assistance to the Jews

At the same time, a number of Polish underground organizations came up with a proposal to develop an organizational structure that would channel all assistance to the Jews. With the approval of Government Delegate Piekalkiewicz, the Council of Assistance to the Jews was established on December 4, 1942 (*Rada Pomocy Zdom*—ZEGOTA). It was headed by Julian Grobelny, a socialist, and had its headquarters in Warsaw. Along with the representatives of various political parties operating underground, the Council also included Leon Feiner (as vice chairman) and Adolf Berman (as secretary). The Council had branches in Krakow, Lwow, Zamosc, and Lublin, and agencies in Radom, Kielce, and Piotrkow. It broadened and improved the existing forms of assistance to Jews living in hiding outside the ghettos by providing them with living quarters, documents, food, medical care, and financial help, and by facilitating communication between members of the same families living in different localities. In Warsaw alone, the Council was taking care of four thousand persons (of these, six hundred were children). Financial means were provided by the Government Delegate. At first, they amounted to half a million zlotys per month, but by November and December 1944, the sum grew to fourteen million zlotys. All in all, ZEGOTA and the Jewish organizations received over a million dollars, 200,000 Swiss francs, and 37,400,000 zlotys. In no other German-occupied country was there an organization like ZEGOTA in existence, though the terror directed against the Aryan populations of these countries was nowhere near as extreme as in Poland.

The growing pace of the extermination campaign prompted the Directorate of Civil Resistance to issue the following proclamation, dated September 17, 1942:

> The tragic fate that befell the Polish people, decimated by the foe, is now compounded by the monstrous, planned slaughter of the Jews that has been carried on in our country for nearly a year. These mass murders are without precedent in the history of the world, and all the cruelties known to man pale beside them. Infants, children, young people, men and women, whether of Catholic or of the Hebrew faith, are being mercilessly murdered, poisoned by gas, buried alive, thrown out of windows onto the pavements below—for no other reason but that they are Jewish; even before death, they suffer the tortures of slow agony, the hell of humiliation and tor-

ment, the cynical sadism of their executioners. More than a million victims have already been slaughtered, and their number grows with each passing day.

Unable to counteract these crimes, the Directorate of Civil Resistance protests in the name of the entire Polish nation against the atrocities perpetrated on the Jews. All Polish political and civic groups join in this protest. As in the case of Polish victims of German persecution, the executioners and their henchmen will be held directly responsible for these crimes.

The Directorate of Civil Resistance

This proclamation was published by the entire underground press and transmitted to London, where it was repeated by the BBC, SWIT, and other Allied radio stations.

Another proclamation was issued by the Directorate of Civil Resistance on March 18, 1943, to counteract the blackmail of Poles who were sheltering Jews:

The Directorate of Civil Resistance makes the following announcement:

The Polish people, themselves the victims of a horrible reign of terror, are witnessing with horror and compassion the slaughter of the remnants of the Jewish population in Poland. Their protest against this crime has reached the ear of the free world. Their effective assistance to Jews escaping from ghettos or extermination camps prompted the German occupiers to publish a decree, threatening with death all Poles who render help to Jews in hiding. Nevertheless, some individuals, devoid of honor and conscience and recruited from the criminal world, have now discovered a new, impious source of profit in blackmailing the Poles who shelter Jews, and the Jews themselves.

The Directorate of Civil Resistance warns that every instance of such blackmail will be recorded and prosecuted with all the severity of the law—right away, whenever possible, but, in any event, in the future.

In accordance with instructions of the Directorate of Civil Resistance, following the publication of the proclamation the underground courts passed a number of death sentences. Underground papers carried the announcement whenever such sentences were carried out (by shooting), and so did the radio. The following Poles were shot for persecuting the Jews: Boguslaw alias Borys Pilnik, Warsaw; Antoni Rozmus, a platoon leader in the criminal police in Warsaw; Jan Grabiec, Krakow; Waclaw Noworol, Lipnica Wielka; Tadeusz Stefan Karcz, Warsaw; Franciszek Sokolowski, Podkowa Lesna; Antoni Pajor, Dobranowice; Janusz Krystek, Grebkow; Jan Lakinski, Warsaw; Boleslaw Szostak, Warsaw; and Antoni Pietrzak, Warsaw.

In urgent cases, when a delay could imperil the safety of Jews who were in hiding, as well as their protectors, the Government Delegate authorized by his decree of February 7, 1944, immediate liquidation of blackmailers and informers, without court sentence, but on orders of the local underground authorities— usually the local chief of Civil Resistance. For instance, a local commander, Witold Rudnicki, ordered the shooting without a court sentence of four blackmailers threatening to betray Jews hiding in Pustelnik near Warsaw.

Considerably earlier—beginning with July 1942—the Directorate of Civil Resistance began to inform the government in London regularly about each new step-up in the persecution of the Jews. Chiefs of the Jewish sections of the Government Delegacy and the High Command of the Home Army provided the Directorate of Civil Resistance with up-to-date information on the developments.

Unfortunately, the first dispatches—including the information that the liquidation of the Warsaw ghetto was begun on July 22, 1942—were disbelieved in London, where they were taken for exaggerated anti-German propaganda.

July 26, 1942. The Germans commenced the liquidation of the Warsaw ghetto. Wall posters ordered the deportation to the east of 6,000 persons, each allowed 15 kilograms of personal effects plus valuables. Departures include to date two trainloads, obviously scheduled for execution. There is despair and suicide. Polish police were removed, to be replaced by Lithuanians, Latvians, and Ukrainians. Summary shootings in homes and streets are common. Dr. Raszej, professor at Poznan University, was killed during consultation with a Jewish physician and patient.

Only when the British intelligence service confirmed this information some months later was the proper use made of dispatches of the Directorate of Civil Resistance.

Samples of the more important messages from the chief of the Directorate of Civil Resistance, Stefan Korbonski (pseudonym: Nowak), are given below. The first pertains to a little-known incident—the first armed encounter in the Warsaw ghetto, three months before the outbreak of the Ghetto Uprising:

January 29, 1943. In recent days, Jews in the Warsaw ghetto defended themselves arms in hand and killed a few Germans. The Jewish National Committee requests that this information be passed on to the Histadrut in Palestine.

March 18, 1943. Remnants of Jews in Radomsk, Ujazd, Sobolew, Radzymin, and Szczerzec near Lwow have been liquidated.

March 23, 1943. Tests with sterilization of women are being conducted in Auschwitz. New crematoria have a capacity of 3,000 persons per day, mostly Jews.

March 30, 1943. On March 13, 14, and 15 trucks loaded with Jews left the Krakow ghetto en route to Auschwitz. About 1,000 people were killed in the ghetto. Jews from Lodz are being taken in the direction of Ozorkow and exterminated there.

May 8, 1943. They are finishing off the ghetto. Two hundred houses were burnt down. The members of the Jewish Council, held since April 19 as hostages, were shot. They were: the chairman Lichtenbaum, the deputy chairman Gustaw Wielikowski, Alfred Sztocman, and Stanislaw Szereszewski. Their bodies were thrown into a pile of garbage.

June 3, 1943. Broadcast repeatedly instructions of the Directorate of Civil Resistance on helping Jews in hiding.

June 10, 1943. In Auschwitz, Bloc X scheduled to become experimental station of the Central Institute of Hygiene from Berlin. Castration, sterilization, and artificial insemination. At present, there are 200 Jewish men and 25 Jewish women there.

July 28, 1943. In Lwow, there are still about 4,000 Jews gathered in the labor camp at Janowskie. During the roll call each morning, two rabbis are forced to fox-trot before the inmates assembled, to the tune of a Jewish band.

August 31, 1943. Liquidation of Jews in Bedzin started at the beginning of this month. About 7,000 were taken to Auschwitz. The young are liquidated first. As of July 1 of this year, the total number of Jews in Poland—including those in the camps, in the ghettos, and in hiding—is 250–300 thousand. Of these, 15,000 are in Warsaw; 80,000 in Lodz; 30,000 in Bedzin; 12,000 in Wilno; 20,000 in Bialystok; 8,000 in Krakow; 4,000 in Lublin; 5,000 in Lwow.

September 23, 1943. The Bedzin ghetto has been liquidated. The Germans murdered 30,000 people.

November 19, 1943. Slaughter of Jews in Trawniki goes on. Massacres also in Poniatowa and Lwow.

June 20, 1944. Beginning with May 15, mass murders are carried out in Auschwitz. Jews are taken first, then the Soviet prisoners of war, and the so-called sick. Mass transports of Hungarian Jews arrive. Thirteen trains per day, 40–50 cars each. Victims convinced they'll be exchanged for POWs or resettled in the east. Gas chambers working round the clock. Corpses are burned in crematoria and out in the open. Over 100,000 people gassed up till now.

July 19, 1944. Murder of Jews in Auschwitz is directed by camp's commander Hoess—read: Hess—and his aide, Grabner.

Mission of Emissary Jan Karski

The Government Delegate also sounded the alarm repeatedly, sending dispatches on the extermination of Jews and transmitting to London messages from Leon Feiner and Adolph Berman, addressed to Rabbi Stephen Wise and Rabbi Nachum Goldman in the United States, and to the two Jewish members of the National Council in London—Ignacy Schwartzbart, a Zionist, and Szmul Zygielbojm, member of BUND. What was even more important, however, was that an eyewitness, emissary Jan Karski, was sent to London. Dressed as an Estonian guard, Karski bribed his way right into the Belzec death camp for Jews and saw everything with Feiner and Berman, who gave him the following instructions:

"We want you to tell the Polish government, the Allied governments, and Allied leaders that we are helpless against the German criminals. We cannot defend ourselves, and no one in Poland can possibly defend us. The Polish underground authorities can save some of us, but they cannot save the masses.

The Germans do not try to enslave us, the way they do other peoples. We are being systematically murdered. . . . All Jews in Poland will perish. It is possible that some few will be saved. But three millions of Polish Jews are doomed to extinction.

"There is no power in Poland able to forestall this fact; neither the Polish nor the Jewish underground can do it. You have to place the responsibility squarely on the shoulders of the Allies. No leader of the United Nations should ever be able to say that he did not know that we were being murdered in Poland and that only outside assistance could help us."

Overcoming tremendous obstacles, Karski reached London in November 1942. He not only informed the Polish government-in-exile and its Premier, General Sikorski, about the genocide in Poland, but also saw personally the following: Foreign Secretary Anthony Eden; leader of the Labour Party Arthur Greenwood; Lord Selbourne; Lord Cranborne; the chairman of the Board of Trade, Hugh Dalton; member of the House of Commons Ellen Wilkinson; British Ambassador to the government-in-exile O'Malley; American Ambassador to the government-in-exile Anthony Drexel Biddle; and Foreign Affairs Undersecretary Richard Law. Karski also testified regarding the extermination of Jews before the UN War Crimes Commission, chaired by Sir Cecil Hurst. Finally, he gave numerous interviews to the British press and also briefed other members of Parliament and organizations of British writers and intellectuals.

Leaving for the United States, Karski then personally told the story of Jews in Poland to the Undersecretary of State, Adolf Berle, Attorney General Biddle, Supreme Court Justice Felix Frankfurter, Archbishops Mooney and Stritch, and American-Jewish leaders such as Stephen Wise, Nachum Goldman, and Waldman. Karski was also received by President Franklin D. Roosevelt, who kept on asking specific questions about the extermination of Jews in Poland long past the time allotted for Karski's audience.

The Polish underground emissary accomplished his mission and passed on to Allied leaders the message about the fate of

Jews in Poland. But, to all practical purposes, his mission produced no results.

Demands for Retaliation

As far as the Polish circles were concerned, one result of Karski's mission was the resolution, passed by the National Council on November 27, 1942, appealing to all Allied nations to undertake a joint action against the extermination of Jews in Poland. Also, on December 10, 1942, the Polish Minister of Foreign Affairs addressed a note to the Allied governments, in which he presented the chronology of specific stages of extermination of Jews in Poland and appealed to Allied governments to "devise effective measures likely to restrain the Germans from further mass extermination." Seven days later, on December 17, 1942, twelve Allied governments issued a joint communiqué, announcing that persons responsible for the extermination of Jews would be punished. No other action was taken, however, despite the fact that the Government Delegate in Poland and the High Command of the Home Army demanded retaliatory bombing of German cities, accompanied by an announcement that the bombing raids were carried out in retaliation for the extermination of Jews. Underground leaders reasoned that British bombardment of German cities was already underway to a certain extent, anyway, in accordance with Churchill's statement of 1940, announcing retaliation for the bombardment of British cities. The only difference would have consisted in scattering appropriate leaflets over the target cities and broadcasting announcements of a general nature, without naming the cities to be bombed. The Polish underground leaders also requested regular bombing missions to destroy all railroad lines leading to extermination camps to prevent further transports from the ghettos. The two Jewish representatives, Feiner and Berman, made similar demands in their dispatches to London. An anti-Nazi SS officer, Kurt Gerstein, recommended the same course of action in his conversation with Swedish diplomat von Otter, aboard the Berlin express. In his dispatch to the government dated June 17, 1943, the chief of the Directorate of Civil Resistance Korbonski summed up the demands for retaliation as follows:

"Public opinion here demands that the attention of the Anglo-Saxon would turn to Poland and calls for retaliations against the Reich, in line with the postulate, reiterated over the past year, of listing the crimes responsible for the bombardments of Germany. . . . I beg and urge that appropriate declarations be made simultaneously with bombing raids over the Reich that these are in retaliation for the latest German bestialities."

No such action was undertaken, however, supposedly because of the technical impossibility of such long-distance flights. And yet, Sir Arthur Harris, chief of the British Bomber Command, considered the bombing of Auschwitz, for instance, technically feasible if carried out from bases in Italy. Captain Leonard Cheshire, V.C., held a similar opinion. Moreover, since bombing raids could have been made on factories around Auschwitz, nothing should have prevented the bombardment of railroad lines bringing fodder for the gas chambers of the largest of German death camps.

Uprising in the Warsaw Ghetto

Beginning with January 1943, officers of the Home Army and representatives of the Jewish Fighting Organization held meetings to plan for a joint action on both sides of the ghetto walls at the outbreak of the uprising. Three Polish units led by Captain Jozef Pszenny (pseudonym: Chwacki), were to break through the ghetto walls, attacking the Germans on the Aryan side and blowing up the walls with explosives. Since it was assumed from the start that the Ghetto Uprising must inevitably end in disaster, this action was planned only to open the way for the retreat of the Jewish fighters.

At this time the Home Army delivered to the Jewish Fighting Organization 1 light machine gun, 2 submachine guns, 50 handguns (all with magazines and ammunition), 10 rifles, 600 hand grenades with detonators, 30 kilograms of explosives (plastic, received from the air drops), 120 kilograms of explosives of own production, 400 detonators for bombs and grenades, 30 kilograms of potassium to make the incendiary "Molotov cocktails," and, finally, great quantities of saltpeter needed to manufacture gun powder. The Jewish Fighting Organization also received instructions on how to manufacture bombs, hand grenades, and incendiary bottles; how to build strongholds; and where to get rails and cement for their construction.

On April 19, 1943—the first day of uprising in the Warsaw ghetto—three Home Army units, commanded by Captain Jozef Pszenny, took up their posts near the ghetto walls on Bonifraterska Street and attempted to blow up the wall with mines. Detected prematurely, they attacked the Germans, while four sappers tried to get to the wall. Unfortunately, two of them were killed on the spot—Eugeniusz Morawski and Jozef Wilk—while a third sustained wounds in both legs. Captain Pszenny ordered his men to retreat and withdrew, taking along four wounded men and detonating the mines on the street. The explosion tore to shreds the bodies of Morawski and Wilk. Several Germans were killed during the engagement, but the attempt to blow up the wall ended in failure.

The next day, a unit of the People's Guard of the Polish Workers Party, led by Franciszek Bartoszek, attacked the German machine-gun posts near the ghetto wall on Nowiniarska Street. Two SS men were killed.

On April 22, a detachment of the Home Army, commanded by Wieckowski, routed a unit of the Lithuanian auxiliary police near the ghetto walls.

On Good Friday, April 23, a Home Army unit led by Lt. Jerzy Skupienski, attacked the gate in the ghetto wall at Pawia Street. They had orders to blow up the gate. Two German sentries were killed at the gate, but—under the heavy barrage of fire from

Germans converging from all sides—the Home Army soldiers had to withdraw, killing on the way four SS and police officers whose car happened to cross their path of retreat.

In harassing actions, ordered by Colonel Antoni Chrusciel (pseudonym: Monter), the Home Army commander of Warsaw, German sentries on Leszno and Orla streets were shot by Home Army soldiers led by Cadet Officer Zbigniew Stalkowski. Another unit of the Home Army, led by Tadeusz Kern-Jedrychowski, killed SS sentries on Zakroczymska Street.

There was also fighting in the area of the Powazki Cemetery (under the command of Wladyslaw Andrzejczak) and near the Jewish cemetery (under Leszek Raabe, commander of the Socialist Fighting Organization). Raabe's deputy, Wlodzimierz Kaczanowski, organized the escape of the Jewish members of the Polish Socialist Party from the ghetto.

On Good Friday, April 23, the Jewish Fighting Organization issued an appeal to the Polish population, declaring that the struggle in the ghetto upheld the time-honored Polish motto: "For your freedom and ours," and stressing that the Jews and the Poles had become brothers in arms.

A particularly daring action was undertaken by a unit of the Corps for Security, under the command of Captain Henryk Iwanski. From the very first days of the Warsaw ghetto's existence, Captain Iwanski's brother, Waclaw, and his two sons—Zbigniew and Roman—maintained regular contact with the Jewish Military Union, providing them with arms, ammunition, and instructional materials smuggled through the sewers or in carts that brought lime and cement into the ghetto. When the uprising began, a unit of the Jewish Military Union occupied positions on Muranowski Square, which was to become the scene of bloodiest fighting. On the first day of the uprising, a Polish and a Jewish flag were raised over this sector. They were clearly visible from the Aryan side and created a deep impression on the Polish population of Warsaw. The commander of the Jewish unit on Muranowski Square, Dawid Moyrc Apfelbaum, sent a message to Captain Iwanski informing him that he had been wounded and asking for arms and ammunition. The next day, Iwanski and eighteen of his men (among them, his brother Waclaw and his two sons, Roman and Zbigniew) made their way into the ghetto by way of a tunnel dug from the cellar of a house at 6 Muranowska Street, on the opposite side and behind the ghetto wall which, at this point, ran in the middle of Muranowska Street. They brought with them arms, ammunition, and food for Apfelbaum's men and, seeing the utter exhaustion of the Jewish fighters, relieved them at their posts amid the ruins on Muranowski Square and Nalewki Street, repelling repeated German attacks. The same tunnel was used without delay to evacuate the Jewish wounded to the Aryan side. Later on, Iwanski's brother and both his sons were killed during the fighting, and Iwanski himself was seriously wounded. After the collapse of the uprising, Iwanski's men carried their wounded commander back through the tunnel, taking along also thirty-four Jewish fighters, fully armed.

After the war, Henryk Iwanski and his wife Wiktoria (who provided shelter and hiding places for the Jews throughout the war) were decorated—along with ten other people—by the Israeli Ambassador in Warsaw, Dov Satoath, with the medal of Yad Vashem.

This was not an isolated instance of the Jews and the Poles fighting together. According to the underground paper *Glos Warszawy* (April 23, 1943), when the uprising began "there were Poles in the ghetto, fighting shoulder to shoulder with the Jews in the streets of the ghetto against the Germans."

In his 100-page report, SS and police general Jürgen Stroop, commander of the German forces fighting in the ghetto, confirmed the fact of Polish diversionary operations and Polish participation in the fighting, both within and without the ghetto. He wrote that his soldiers were "constantly under fire from outside of the ghetto, i.e., from the Aryan side"; he described Iwanski's action as follows: "The main Jewish group, with some Polish bandits mixed in, retreated to the so-called Muranowski Square already in the course of the first or the second day of fighting. It was reinforced there by several more Polish bandits."

A little over a year later, during the Warsaw Rising, a detachment of the Jewish Fighting Organization joined the ranks of the Home Army in the struggle against the Germans. The Jewish fighters were commanded by Icek Cukierman, once deputy and contact man on the Aryan side, for Mordecai Anielewicz, commander of the Jewish Fighting Organization.

It was during the Warsaw Uprising, too, that the Grey Ranks—composed of boy scouts and led by Lt. Colonel Jan Mazurkiewicz (pseudonym: Radoslaw)—seized, in what once had been the ghetto, the labor camp still maintained by the Germans for Jews, whose lives had been spared so they could work at tearing down whatever remained of the burned ghetto, but who were also doomed to die. They freed 358 Jews who joined Radoslaw's units enthusiastically. Later, most of them were killed, together with those who had freed them. When Radoslaw was wounded in both legs, but still continued in command, it was the Jews who carried his stretcher, often through the underground passages in the city sewers.

A question arises, Should the Home Army have helped the Jews with more than arms, diversionary actions, and efforts to open up escape routes for the Jewish fighters? The answer must be negative. Not even the entire strength of the Home Army in Warsaw could have saved the ghetto or brought victory. There was considerable concentration of German army, SS, and gendarmerie forces in Warsaw and vicinity, which would have been sent into action immediately, with but one possible outcome—a crushing defeat of both the Jewish Fighting Organization and the Home Army. An uprising in the ghetto could have been more than a heroic and tragic gesture of protest and self-defense only if the Soviet army could have come to the rescue in time to win victory. The only other alternative would have been a total disarray of the German armies. But in April 1943, the Soviets were hundreds of miles away from Warsaw and the German armies showed no signs of decay, fighting doggedly on all war fronts.

Throughout the Ghetto Uprising, daily reports on the course of the fighting were transmitted by the chief of the Directorate of Civil Resistance Korbonski to the radio station SWIT, which based its broadcasts on their contents. Below are some samples of these messages:

April 20, 1943. Yesterday the Germans began the liquidation of 35,000 in our ghetto. The Jews are defending themselves. We can hear shots and explosions of grenades. The Germans are using tanks and armored cars. They have losses. There are fires in several places. Speak to the ghetto today.

April 21, 1943. The fighting in the ghetto continues. Throughout the night we could hear shots, explosions, and fires.

April 28, 1943. Fighting continues in the ghetto. The Germans are burning houses systematically, one after another.

May 7, 1943. *Rzeczpospolita* of May 6 contains a statement of the Government Delegate, denouncing German crimes in the ghetto. He pays homage to the Jewish fighters, voices our solidarity, and calls on all Poles to help those who escape from the ghetto.

May 15, 1943. The horrible massacre of the remnants of the Warsaw ghetto has been going on for three weeks now. Led by the Jewish Fighting Organization, the Jews defended themselves heroically, arms in hand. The Germans used artillery and armored cars. Over 300 Germans have been killed by the Jewish fighters; some 1,000 Germans have been wounded. Tens of thousands of Jews have been deported, murdered, or burned alive by the Germans.

May 22, 1943. A rumor circulates among the Germans that the Gestapo chief in Warsaw, Dr. von Sammern, who had been recalled, was sentenced to death for the disgrace suffered by the Germans because of the armed resistance in the ghetto.

June 9, 1943. The underground *Economic Bulletin* reports on May 15 that 100,000 living units, 2,000 industrial locations, 3,000 commercial establishments and several factories have been burned or blown up in the Warsaw ghetto. In September 1939 only 78,000 living units were destroyed in the entire city of Warsaw.

June 29, 1943. All inhabitants of the ghettos in Stanislawow, Lukow, Wegrow, and Zolkiew have been murdered. In Warsaw, some 2,000 Jews are breathing their last in cellars and ruins. There is still some fighting during the nights. At Sobibor, German bands playing at the station greet Jews arriving from abroad.

In his letter to Cukierman, dated April 23, 1943, Mordecai Anielewicz refers to the first of the above dispatches, on which the SWIT broadcast was based:

The fact that . . . the radio station SWIT broadcasts a beautiful program about our struggle (which we heard on our set here), was the source of great satisfaction. It gives us courage in our fight to know that we are not forgotten on the other side of the ghetto wall.

Government Delegate Jankowski also sent urgent dispatches to the Polish government in London, beginning with April 21, 1943.

Meanwhile in London, Szmul Zygielbojm, a member of the Polish National Council, committed suicide on May 13, 1943, in protest of the indifference of the Allies to the sufferings of the Warsaw ghetto. He explained the reason for his action in letters addressed to the president of the Polish Republic, Wladyslaw Raczkiewicz, and to the premier of the government-in-exile, General Wladyslaw Sikorski.

Jewish Partisan Units

Towards the end of the Ghetto Uprising, there began an organized evacuation of the Jewish fighters. It was not free from tragic mistakes, such as the suicide of Mordecai Anielewicz and his staff in the bunker at 18 Mila Street, despite the fact that there was a way for them to escape, which was discovered later by others. Jewish fighters escaped through tunnels dug from cellar to cellar and through the city sewers. Members of friendly Polish organizations, such as the Socialist Fighting Organization, awaited them on the Aryan side with trucks, which transported the rescued Jews to the woods near Warsaw. On April 29, for instance, soldiers of the People's Guard, led by Lieutenant Wladyslaw Gaik, organized the escape of forty men of the Jewish Fighting Organization, fully armed, and took them to the woods in the vicinity of Wyszkow. The same operation was repeated again on May 10, when another thirty Jewish fighters were rescued, joining the others and forming a partisan group named after Mordecai Anielewicz. Other Jewish partisan units were formed, often named after Polish national heroes. In the Lublin district, for instance, there were Jewish partisan groups, commanded by Samuel Jegier and named after Emilia Plater (a heroine of the Insurrection of 1831) and Jan Kozietulski (a hero of the Napoleonic wars). One of the partisan groups, led by Chil Grynszpan, was named after Berek Joselewicz, a Jew and a colonel in the Polish armies during the Insurrection of 1794. Another partisan group was composed of Polish peasants from the village of Polichno, but had a Jewish commanding officer, using the pseudonym of "Szymek." When he was killed in action, the peasants buried him in a Catholic cemetery as a sign of their respect. Among still other partisan groups, there was a Jewish unit commanded by Mieczyslaw Gruber; a mixed Polish-Jewish unit under the command of a Jewish veterinarian, Dr. Mieczyslaw Skotnicki, which operated in the woods near Parczew; and in the Radom district, a group led by Julian Ajzenman-Kaniewski (pseudonym: Chytry). Small bands of stragglers usually joined the first partisan unit they met, and many of them fought together with the Home Army partisans.

Other Jews, who managed to survive the uprising in the ghetto and to escape through tunnels and sewers to the Aryan side, fared much worse. The most fortunate among them made their way to the forests and either joined the partisans hiding there or set up camps under the partisans' protection. The rest were swept into the nets of special manhunts, conducted by the Germans, or blended with the Polish population which—spurred on by three successive appeals of the Council of Assistance to the Jews (ZEGOTA), an appeal from General Sikorski (May 5, 1943), and an appeal from the Government Delegate Jankowski (May 6, 1943)—was doing all it could to save the tragic remnants. At the same time, ZEGOTA requested that the Polish government-in-exile take steps to initiate an international agreement in an effort to save the remaining Jews through exchange or some other means. However, no such agreement was ever concluded.

Also at that time, three publications printed by the underground presses reached London: *Before the Eyes of the World*, a book by Maria Kann, presented the story of the Warsaw ghetto and the Ghetto Uprising; *One Year in Treblinka*, a booklet written by Jankiel Wiernik, an escape from the death camp; and a volume of poems entitled *From the Abyss,* the work of eleven Jewish poets. These books created a deep impression in the West—and that was the end of it.

This state of affairs lasted until the German armies, defeated by the Soviets, began their retreat.

Polish Losses Caused by Helping Jews

Pursuant to paragraph 5 of the Führer's decree of October 12, 1939, Governor Hans Frank issued the ordinance of October 15, 1941, and several others which imposed the death penalty for Poles who would give shelter to the Jews or otherwise assist them by transporting them, giving or selling them food, failing to report Jews in hiding, handing them a piece of bread or a glass of water, and so forth. The usual penalty was execution by firing squad or hanging. Another form of punishment was the burning of the home in which the Jews were sheltered, together with the entire family of its owners, including children and casual visitors as well as livestock. Among those punished for helping Jews were peasants, workers, and members of the clergy and other professions such as professors and doctors. In the case of mixed Polish-Jewish couples, both man and wife were executed and their bodies buried at random or in Jewish cemeteries.

Among the numerous cases were (1) a postman named Semik, who knew German and spoke in that language in the defense of a Jewish couple; (2) a Pole who protested against the mass execution of Jews, which he was ordered to witness; (3) another Pole who handed a bucket of water to Jews in a locked railway carriage taking them to an extermination camp; (4) a Pole who tried to toss a sack of bread over the ghetto wall; and (5) the Polish policeman Klis, who helped Jews forge identity cards.

There are no complete data as to the number of Poles murdered by the Germans for giving shelter to the Jews or helping them in other ways. There are, however, many fragmentary reports pertaining to specific instances, for example, an announcement of the SS and police commander in the district of Galicja (January 28, 1944) listing the names of five Poles sentenced to death for helping the Jews. Widely known was the case of a gardener, Ludomir Marczak, and his family, who were shot in the Pawiak Prison on March 7, 1944, for hiding in a dugout in their garden about thirty Jews—among them, Emanuel Ringelblum, the chronicler of the Ghetto Uprising, who perished with the others. Between September 13, 1942, and May 25, 1944, about two hundred peasants were shot or burned alive in the Kielce district in reprisal for helping the Jews. The same fate befell seventeen persons in the Krakow district. In the cemetery of the town of Nowy Sacz, between three hundred and five hundred Jews and Poles were shot between 1939 and August 1942—the Poles for sheltering the Jews. The same reason accounted for the execution of forty Poles in the Lublin district, forty-seven in the Rzeszow district, and nineteen in the Warsaw district. In the Lwow district, nearly a thousand inhabitants of the city of Lwow were punished with death in the Belsen camp for having helped the Jews. Witnesses during the Eichmann trial also referred to several individual cases (e.g., Dr. Jozef Barzminski).

A dispatch from the chief of the Directorate of Civil Resistance Korbonski illustrates one case:

> May 3, 1943. In Mszana Dolna, on March 22, *Volksdeutsch* Gelb hanged a peasant by his feet and tormented him to death for having sold potatoes to a Jew.

Still, most of the Poles who had been helping the Jews survived the war and the German persecutions. Today they are frequently in touch with the Jewish families they have helped, visiting them in Israel, in the United States, and in other countries, and even settling in Israel at the invitation of the Jewish families living there. In the Avenue of the Righteous in Jerusalem, most of the plaques commemorating those who saved Jews bear Polish names. According to the brochure entitled *Las Sprawiedliwych* (The Forest of Righteous), published by Szymon

Datner, director of the Jewish Historical Institute in Warsaw, the Institute listed up to April 1968 the names of 343 Poles murdered for helping the Jews. However, the names of 101 additional victims the Institute was unable to identify.

Among the Polish masses who tried to save as many Jews as possible, there were also exceptions other than the blackmailers and the informers, whom the Polish underground punished with death. Partisan units of the fascist fraction of the National Armed Forces hunted down the Jews hiding in the forests. They were also responsible for the killing in Warsaw of two officers of the High Command of the Home Army who were of Jewish origin—Jerzy Makowiecki, an engineer, and Ludwik Widerszal.

On the other hand, some prominent and outspoken prewar anti-Semites—such as the leader of the radical right ONR, Jan Mosdorf; editor of the weekly *Prosto z mostu*, Stanislaw Piasecki; or the well-known journalist Adolf Nowaczynski—changed completely. Mosdorf did everything in his power to help the Jews in the Auschwitz camp, and he died together with the Jews. Piasecki and Nowaczynski became the champions of the persecuted Jews.

A surviving leading representative of the Jews, Adolf Berman, now living in Tel Aviv, appraised the role played by the Poles as follows:

> Descriptions of the Jewish martyrdom in Poland often dwell on sufferings inflicted upon the hunted Jews by Polish blackmailers and informers, by the "blue" police, by fascist hooligans and other scum of the society. Far less is being written about the fact that thousands of Poles put their own lives in jeopardy to help the Jews. It is much easier to see the foul scum and flotsam on a river than to discern the deep, clear current under its surface. But the current was there. . . .
> Time will come when we will have a great Golden Book of Poles who, in that hideous "time of contempt" held out a brother's hand to the Jews, saved Jews from death, and became a symbol of humanitarianism and the brotherhood of peoples to the Jewish underground movement.

We noted at the beginning of this chapter that full statistics on the Poles killed by the Germans for helping Jews are not available. A token contribution was made by the figures published so far by the Jewish Historical Institute in Warsaw, which up to April 1968 identified 343 Poles executed by the Germans for assisting Jews. Twenty years have passed since then, and no progress seems to have been made in researching the problem. There is reason to believe that the Institute was staffed by Jews hostile to the Poles, who preferred the role of prosecutor to that of judge, hence the negligible results of the search for cases of Jews saved by Poles. It is also probable that after the publication of the fragmentary data in 1968, certain Jewish circles used their influence to stop the further activities of the Institute in that area.

The task has been taken up, however, by two other organizations: the Association of Former Political Prisoners, mostly inmates of Auschwitz, which estimates the number of Poles murdered for helping the Jews at 2,500; and the Maximilian Kolbe Foundation. Its publication *Martyrs of Charity* has identified so far by name 2,300 Poles executed for their help to the Jews. The author of the study, Waclaw Zajaczkowski, was awarded the Yad Vashem medal, for several members of his family were executed for helping Jews.

What were the penalties for helping Jews in other countries? In Norway, which had about 2,000 Jews, not a single case was recorded. In Denmark, one man by the name of Heiteren was killed while helping the boarding by the Jews of the ferryboat taking them to Sweden. The total number of Jews in Denmark was 6,000.

In Holland, which had 140,000 Jews, persons who helped them were sent to concentration camps and their estates impounded. In Belgium, which was the home of 90,000 Jews, several thousand were hidden by Gentiles, but there were no arrests of Belgians for that offense. In France, which had 270,000 Jews, the French who helped them were interned in a camp, and some priests in the diocese of Lyons were arrested for hiding Jewish children. In Italy (an ally of Germany), which had 50,000 Jews, there were anti-Jewish regulations, but they did not include genocide. When the Mussolini government was overthrown on July 25, 1943, and replaced by that of Marshal Badoglio, the Germans started an "action" against the Jews immediately in the part of Italy under their control; but many of them went into hiding, including 3,000 sheltered by the Vatican. Not a single Italian was sentenced to death for hiding Jews.

It is obvious that no comparison is possible between the situation in Poland, where about 2,500 Poles were killed for helping the Jews, and western Europe, when in Denmark, Norway, Holland, France, and Italy only one single person, a Dane, was shot while embarking the Jews escaping to Sweden.

Furthermore, in France the Petain-Laval government actively helped to round up the Jews to be sent to the extermination camps, doing so on its own initiative before receiving German orders to that effect. Yet the American Jews level charges of anti-Semitism against the Poles, not the French.

Why Was Poland Chosen the Site of Extermination?

Anti-Semitism of the local population certainly was not the reason for the Nazis' choice of Poland as the main extermination site for the Jews (who were also being murdered in the Reich, e.g., in Dachau, Sachsenhausen, and other camps). Certain segments of the Polish population were, indeed, anti-Semitic, but this changed when the Poles saw the persecution of Jews with their own eyes and when they themselves became subject to deportation, mass arrests, concentration camps, and mass executions. Historians of Jewish persecutions are unanimous in their agreement that, next to the Jews, the Poles were the most oppressed of all nations and were doomed to gradual extermination, in accordance with the General Eastern Plan. Among charges listed in the indictment presented by Gideon Hausner, prosecutor at the Eichmann trial, one (no. 9) was that Eichmann was responsible for the deportation of 500,000 Poles. Eichmann was convicted on this count too, and the sentence assumed he had been motivated by his intention to destroy the intelligentsia class of Polish society.

The real reason why Poland had been chosen was the fact that of all the European Jews marked for extermination, three and a half million were already in Poland. German railroad transportation lines were overburdened because of the war. It was much simpler to build the extermination camps in Poland and to bring in the Polish Jews from nearby areas, rather than transport them by rail to Hungary or France. The largest of these camps, Auschwitz, was established near the German border to shorten the distance for the transports of Jews from Hungary, France, and Italy. After the outbreak of the Soviet-German war, when the transportation problems became even more acute, one and a half million Polish and Russian Jews were murdered by special units, the so-called *Einsatzgruppen*—not in the extermination camps but on the spot, in front of the mass graves they had been forced to dig for themselves.

Transport problems played a role not only in the extermination of the Jews, but also in considerations of ways to save them. In 1942, British Foreign Secretary Anthony Eden told President Franklin D. Roosevelt:

"The whole problem with the Jews in Europe is very difficult and we should move very cautiously about offering to take all Jews out of a country. If we do so, then the Jews of the world will be wanting us to make similiar offers in Poland and Germany. Hitler might take us up on any such offer, and there simply are not enough ships and means of transportation in the world to handle them. . . ."

The Germans also undoubtedly reasoned that this greatest crime in the history of the world might be easier to hide in eastern Europe, cut off from the world by German occupation, than in the west, which—although also under German occupation—could never be isolated effectively from neutral countries like Switzerland, Spain, or even England.

One cannot end an account of the extermination of the Jews

without stating that the guilt of genocide will rest forever on the entire German nation, which—from the first anti-Jewish excesses in prewar Germany and as long as Hitler was winning the war—supported the Führer and identified fully with him and with the Nazi party. Nothing but words—protesting or threatening—came from the Allies, but their responsibility is of an entirely different kind and can in no way be compared to that of the Germans. The sin of commission cannot be compared to the sin of omission.

CHAPTER V

The Jews in Postwar Poland

AFTER THE UNEXPECTED ATTACK OF JUNE 22, 1941, THE GERMAN armies reached within a few months the suburbs of Leningrad in the north, those of Moscow in the center, and the banks of the Volga at Stalingrad. The Germans failed, however, to cross the Volga and cut off the main line of communication between the north and the south of Russia. Several months of heavy fighting culminated in the battle of Stalingrad and the surrender of a 300,000-strong German army on January 31, 1943. It was the turning point of the war and the beginning of the German retreat. The Soviet army reached the Polish border on January 3, 1944, near the town of Sarny.

Stalin remembered well the goals of the October Revolution of 1917, which included entering Poland as the gateway to the defeated and rebellious Germany and the utterly exhausted

France, with a view to spreading the Communist revolution over all of Europe. The first step was the establishment of a Communist government in Poland, and for that purpose a Provisional Polish Revolutionary Committee was formed in Bialystok, already seized by the Red Army. The committee, intended as the first Bolshevik government of Poland, included J. Marchlewski, E. Prochniak, E. Kon, and J. Unszlicht. The Communists underrated the strength of the very recently restored independent Poland, a sovereign state since November 11, 1918. In August 1920 the Soviet army under Marshal Tukhachevski was defeated in the battle of Warsaw by the improvised Polish army commanded by Joseph Pilsudski. The first cavalry army of Semyon Budienny was smashed and fled in disarray. There was on Budienny's staff a young political commissar by the name of Stalin, who was charged with guarding the Communist orthodoxy of the troops. The memory of his desperate flight, chased by Polish lancers, left a deep scar in Stalin's mind.

The defeat near Warsaw put an end to the Soviet plans for a Communist Europe, and a peace treaty between the Soviet Union and the independent Polish government was signed on March 18, 1921, in Riga. It remained in force until the day of September 17, 1939, when the Red Army broke the treaty of Riga by invading Poland. They repeated the invasion on January 4, 1944, when they entered Poland again in pursuit of the German army in retreat.

As soon as Stalin saw that victory over the Germans was within his reach, he revived the master plan which had failed in 1920. He knew that the Germans would leave Poland and be replaced by Soviet soldiers under his command, ready to establish a government of his choice. They would not encounter armed resistance as in 1920, and Poland would be taken over. Yet appearances had to be observed for the benefit of the Western Allies, and that is why Stalin formed on June 10, 1943, in Moscow, a "Union of Polish Patriots" whose members were handpicked by Stalin and were under his orders. Ever since the Soviet defeat of 1920 Stalin hated the Poles. He proved it by ordering the execution of four thousand Polish officers, mostly

The German Commissioner of Ostrowiec, Motschall, signed the announcement, reminding all Poles, "in view of repeated instances of Jews being hidden by Poles" that "anyone who shelters Jews and gives or sells them food will be punished by death. This is the final warning."

In the official journal for the General Government of November 14, 1942, Friedrich Wilhelm Kruger, Secretary of State for Security, signed the police order about the death penalty for anyone giving food or shelter to any Jew.

BEKANNTMACHUNG

Betrifft:
Beherbergung von geflüchteten Juden.

Es besteht Anlass zu folgendem Hinweis:
Gemäss der 3. Verordnung über Aufenthaltsbeschränkungen im Generalgouvernement vom 15. 10. 1941 (VO. Bl. GG. S. 595) unterliegen Juden, die den jüdischen Wohnbezirk unbefugt verlassen, der Todesstrafe.

Gemäss der gleichen Vorschrift unterliegen Personen, die solchen Juden wissentlich Unterschlupf gewähren, Beköstigung verabfolgen oder Nahrungsmittel verkaufen, ebenfalls der Todesstrafe.

Die nichtjüdische Bevölkerung wird daher dringend gewarnt:

1.) Juden Unterschlupf zu gewähren,

2.) Juden Beköstigung zu verabfolgen,

3.) Juden Nahrungsmittel zu verkaufen.

Tschenstochau, den 24. 9. 42.

OGŁOSZENIE

Dotyczy:
przetrzymywania ukrywających się żydów.

Zachodzi potrzeba przypomnienia, że stosownie do § 3 Rozporządzenia o ograniczeniach pobytu w Gen. Gub. z dnia 15. X. 1941 roku (Dz. Rozp. dla GG. str. 595) żydzi, opuszczający dzielnicę żydowską bez zezwolenia, podlegają karze śmierci.

Według tego rozporządzenia, osobom, które takim żydom świadomie udzielają przytułku, dostarczają im jedzenia lub sprzedają artykuły żywnościowe, grozi również kara śmierci.

Niniejszym ostrzega się stanowczo ludność nieżydowską przed:

1.) udzielaniem żydom przytułku,

2.) dostarczaniem im jedzenia,

3.) sprzedawaniem im artykułów żywnościowych.

Częstochowa, dnia 24. 9. 42.

Der Stadthauptmann
Dr. Franke

The German Town Commissioner Dr. Franke announces on September 24, 1942, that it is necessary to remind the Jews that leaving the Jewish quarter without permission is punishable by death, and warns the non-Jewish population that sheltering Jews and giving them food is also punishable by death.

The German County Commissioner for Tarnow, Dr. Pernutz, announces the deportation of the Jews on September 16, 1942, and states that any Pole who shelters a Jew, then or later, will be shot. (Paragraph 3)

Jan Perycz and nine other Poles were shot in December 1943 "for helping bandits, sheltering Jews, possession of weapons, etc."

Stefan Barglik from Tokarnia, near Krakow, was condemned to death for sympathizing with the Jews by giving them shelter.

The Polish underground paper announces the trial and death penalty for Janusz Krystek for killing two Polish citizens of Jewish nationality, and for Boleslaw Szostak for blackmailing Jews by threatening to turn them over to German authorities.

RZECZPOSPOLITA POLSKA

OK IV. NR. 4 (76)   WARSZAWA   26 MARCA 1944 R.

KOMUNIKATY K. W. P.

KOMUNIKAT Nr 32

W dniu 4.III.44 w Warszawie został zlikwidowany bahnschutz Schmalz, degenerat i okrutnik, znęcający się nad Polakami. W starciu zginęło ponadto 5 innych Niemców, utrudniających likwidację Schmalza.

Kierownictwo Walki Podziemnej
9.III.44.

OBWIESZCZENIE

Wyrokiem Sądu Specjalnego Cywilnego Okręgu Warszawskiego z 18.VI. i 30.XI 43 zostali skazani na karę śmierci oraz utratę praw publicznych i obywatelskich praw honorowych:

1) Janusz Krystek, l. 22, pomocnik leśny, zam. gm. Grębków, pow. Sokołów — za zabicie dwóch obywateli polskich narodowości żydowskiej,

2) Jan Malinowski, l. 52, sołtys gromady Szaruty, gm. Ruchna, pow. węgrowski — za gorliwe ściąganie kontyngentów dla okupanta i grożenie ludności denuncjacjami do władz niemieckich o należenie do organizacji.

Wyroki powyższe wykonano przez zastrzelenie.

Kierownictwo Walki Podziemnej
20.II.44.

OBWIESZCZENIE

Wyrokiem Sądu Specjalnego Cywilnego został skazany na karę śmierci oraz utratę praw publicznych i obywatelskich praw honorowych:

Bolesław Szostak, l. 39, płut. służby śledczej w Warszawie — za wymuszanie okupu od obywateli polskich narodowości żydowskiej, pod groźbą oddania w ręce władz niemieckich.

Kierownictwo Walki Podziemnej
9.III.44.

OGŁOSZENIE

Organy Polski Podziemnej podjęły w swoim czasie akcję badania i rejestrowania zbrodni popełnionych przez okupanta w Polsce, w celu pociągnięcia winnych i sprawców tych zbrodni do odpowiedzialności we właściwym czasie.

Akcja ta prowadzona jest obecnie nadal przez specjalnie dla tego celu powołaną Komisję oraz jej odpowiedniki, czynne przy placówkach naszej administracji.

Przypomina się, że powyższą akcją objęci są nie tylko ci spośród okupantów, którzy zajmując kierownicze stanowiska w administracji okupacyjnej ponoszą z tego tytułu odpowiedzialność za wszystkie zbrodnie okupanta, ale również wszyscy pozostający na niższych szczeblach administracyjnej, policyjnej i partyjnej hierarchii okupanta, działający na jego rzecz i w jego imieniu lub korzystający z jego przywilejów z których polecenia bądź inicjatywy lub przy

Zbigniew Lewandoski, pseudonym "Szyna," trained Jewish fighters in the use of explosives. He also took part in various attacks by the Polish Home Army at the ghetto walls, most notably on April 22, 1943, when he killed a number of German policemen.

Captain Jerzy Lewinski, pseudonym "Chuchro," organized support and training for the ghetto fighters preparing to fight. He also organized deliveries of arms and ammunition, and took part in the action of April 22, 1943. He was murdered by the Germans in the ruins of the Warsaw ghetto.

Officer Cadet Zbigniew Stalkowski, pseudonym "Stadnicki," took part in the Home Army attacks at the ghetto walls in April of 1943.

Lieutenant Jozef Pszenny, pseudonym, "Chwacki," took part in the April 19, 1943, attempt to destroy the ghetto wall on Bonifraterska Street.

Jozef Wilk, pseudonym "Orlik," was killed at the ghetto wall in Warsaw when a patrol of the Home Army tried to destroy the wall to help the Jews escape.

Eugeniusz Morawski, pseudonym "Mlodek," died in the action of April 19, 1943, at the ghetto wall.

Zofia Kossak-Szczucka, a well known Polish writer, was one of the initiators of the Zegota Committee.

Julian Grobelny, pseudonym "Trojan," the first chairman of the Council to Aid the Jews.

This is one of the documents in the archives of the Jewish Historical Institute in Warsaw, showing the extensive activities of Zegota (The Council to Aid the Jews). This kind of information was regularly passed on to the Polish Government in London.

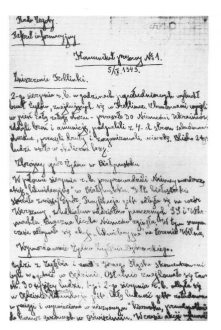

An official notice from the Polish Government in London, dated December 10, 1942, to all Allied Governments.

In 1980 Stefan Korbonski was awarded the Yad Vashem Medal of Honor by the Yad Vashem Martyrs' and Heroes' Remembrance Authority in Jerusalem for saving Jews in World War II.

reservists, who had been taken prisoner in 1939 and whose graves were discovered at Katyn in 1943. Ten thousand other Polish officers were sent to the arctic north of Russia, by the White Sea, never to be heard of again. Most of them were educated men, civil servants or professionals in civilian life. Stalin's aim was to decapitate the Polish nation by exterminating its leadership.

To realize his plan of seizing total control of Poland, Stalin formed two teams: one to satisfy appearances and the Western Allies, the other to actually rule Poland. The first was headed by the Polish Communist Wanda Wasilewska and the other by Jacob Berman, whom Stalin knew well.

The choice of Berman was connected with his Jewish origin, which exonerated him from suspicions of Polish patriotism and advocacy of Poland's independence. Stalin regarded the Jews as cosmopolites, whose loyalties would be to Zionism rather than the country of their residence.

As the situation developed, the Polish Patriots' Union was converted on July 21, 1944, to the "Polish Committee for National Liberation," which formed in Moscow on June 21, 1945, the Provisional Government of National Unity. Out of the twenty-one members of the cabinet, seventeen were Communists or their supporters. Among the four Democrats was Stanislaw Mikolajczyk, a Polish peasant leader and former prime minister of the Polish government in exile in London, who had returned to Poland.

The Jews in the Communist Political Police

The head of the second team, Jacob Berman, who was a Soviet citizen, was camouflaged in the secondary position of under-secretary of state at the Foreign Office and later at the Office of the Cabinet, from which he exerted control over all branches of the government. He had a direct telephone line to the Kremlin and to Stalin himself. That telephone was used on one occasion, after office hours, by William Tonesk, a Polish American who described the event in his interview published in the *New York Polish Daily* of June 9, 1987.

The principal instrument of Berman's power was his total control of the Ministry of State Security, which began—under Stalin's instructions—to liquidate all centers of possible opposition, often by simply murdering persons suspected of advocating Poland's independence, especially former members of the Home Army, which fought the Germans during the occupation.

During the electoral campaign preceding the election of January 19, 1947, the agents of the political police, known as "Bezpieka" (an abbreviation of the "Security") murdered 118 activists of the only independent parties, the Polish Socialist Party and the Peasant Party. The list of their names was published in Stefan Korbonski's book *In the Name of the Kremlin*. The names of ten additional members of the Peasant Party and four of the Polish Socialist Party killed by the Communist political police were published in the periodical *Zeszyty* of the Paris *Kultura*.

The relations between Berman and Stalin are described in the interview he granted to Teresa Toranska, which is published in her important work *Them*. It describes the intimate, sumptuous parties in Stalin's dacha which lasted from 10 P.M. until dawn. On one occasion, when no women were present, Berman waltzed with Molotov, while Stalin turned the gramophone and changed the records.

Berman's career ended in 1957, when he was expelled from the "Polish United Workers' Party" (the Communist Party) by the Bezpieka secret police on charges of "serious infractions of legality." The infractions consisted of the false imprisonment, torture, and murder of thousands of people.

The team assembled by Berman at the beginning of his rule consisted of the following dignitaries, all of them Jewish:

1. General Roman Romkowski (Natan Grünsapau-Kikiel), was vice-minister of State Security. He was a member of the then-illegal Communist Youth Organization and was trained in the Komintern "Lenin School." As vice-minister of State Security, Berman's confidant supervised the departments of investigation,

training, and invigilation. He also managed the secret treasury of the Politbureau, controlled by Jacob Berman, Hilary Minc, and Boleslaw Bierut, a Russified Pole promoted by Stalin. Bierut had served many years as an international agent of the Komintern.

Romkowski alone had access to the three huge built-in safes which contained millions of dollars in cash, gold bars, and diamonds. Romkowski often interrogated prisoners personally, among them Stefan Korbonski. He was active in the faking of the election of January 19, 1947, and conducted the investigation of Wladyslaw Gomulka, of which more will be said later. He was delegated to Budapest in connection with the case of Laszlo Rayk and to Prague in connection with that of Slansky; both Communist leaders were executed for allegedly departing from the party line. After the accession of Gomulka to power, Romkowski was expelled from the Communist Party in April 1955, arrested, and sentenced to fifteen years imprisonment for the "infractions" at the Ministry of State Security.

2. General Julius Hibner, born David Schwartz, was a Communist who had served in the civil war in Spain in the years 1936–1938. He was aide to the minister of State Security, charged with the Border Defense Corps and the Internal Security Corps. In 1951–1956 he was commander of the internal military forces and in 1956–1960 vice-minister of the Interior.

3. Luna Brystygier was director of the fifth department of the Ministry of State Security. Joseph Swiatlo (Licht), a colonel of the security police who defected to the United States on January 5, 1953, testified as follows about Brystygier:

> The official duties of her department include the prosecution of foreign and non-Soviet influences in the Polish political parties other than the communist one, in trade and youth associations. Luna Brystygier is a chapter unto herself. She is now over fifty, rather the worse for wear, as she had a full and eventful life.
>
> She started her career in Lwow, at the time of the entry of the Soviet army in 1939. As the former wife of Dr. Nathan Brystygier, a Zionist activist in the pre-war period, Luna had all the required contacts and connections. Immediately after the arrival of the Red Army in Lwow in 1939 Brystygier started denouncing people on such a scale that she antagonized even some communist party mem-

bers. That was the beginning of her feud with colonel Rozanski, now the director of the investigation department of the "Bezpieka" political police. At that time she, Rozanski and Borejsza (Rozanski's brother) competed in denouncing people to the N.K.V.D. (now known as the K.G.B.). There was sharp rivalry between them in that area. Eager to win, Brystygier wrote to the N.K.V.D. a report accusing Rozanski of being a member of a Zionist family. It was true that his father, Dr. Goldberg, was before the war editor of the Zionist newspaper "Haynt." Rozanski knew about that report and I recall him complaining: "Just think, comrade, that . . . squealed on me! But comrade Luna forgets that I have had a longer career in the N.K.V.D. than she." Rozanski did have a long record of work for the N.K.V.D. and that is why he still holds his job.

After the entry of the Red Army in Lwow Brystygier conducted her activity as an informer by organizing the so-called Committee for Political Prisoners. That committee was instrumental in helping the N.K.V.D. to capture party deviants and that was how Brystygier finished off some of the comrades. She has now a very strong position at the "Bezpieka" headquarters. They call her the fifty vice-minister of State Security. The reason is quite simple: during her stay in Russia Brystygier was for a long time simultaneously the mistress of Berman, Minc and Szyr. The first two have especially strong commitments to her. That is why whenever Brystygier wants to carry through anything in the Ministry of State Security, even in opposition to her ostensible bosses Radkiewicz and Romkowski, she always has her way. Many times Radkiewicz did not even have the time to submit a proposal to Bierut when Bierut himself or Berman called him and said: "Listen, you have on your desk such and such. Why didn't you tell us about it?" They knew everything before it was referred by Radkiewicz, because Brystygier tells them these things at night. Beautiful, eh comrade Thomas? But it is through you and your closest collaborators, Berman and Minc, that she wields such power. . . .

4. Colonel Anatol Fejgin was director of the tenth department of the Ministry of State Security. His job was the tracing and liquidation of all Western influences and the collection of damaging material about Party members, with the exception of Bierut. After the arrest of Wladyslaw Gomulka in July 1951 (he was released in December 1954) and the defection to the West on December 5, 1953, of his deputy, the colonel of security police Joseph Swiatlo (Licht), Fejgin was arrested in April 1955 and sentenced to fifteen years in prison.

5. The security police colonel Joseph Swiatlo was in his youth a member of the Union of Young Communists. He joined in 1942 the army formed in Russia by Berling and was assigned to security work, where he met his old friend from the Communist organization, Romkowski. He was transferred to the Ministry of State Security (the equivalent in Poland of the K.G.B.) and appointed deputy director of the tenth department headed by Colonel Anatol Fejgin. Because of his connection with Romkowski, Swiatlo had actually a stronger position than Fejgin, with a direct line to Moscow and the right of access to Stalin's right hand, Beria himself. Two massive steel closets in his office contained material which incriminated every important personality from Berman down and was kept for purposes of blackmail. In 1953 Swiatlo realized that he knew too much to get out alive from his position, and during a visit in West Berlin he defected to the United States on December 5, 1953, and was in Washington D.C. on December 23, 1953.

During ten months of interrogation Swiatlo revealed everything he knew. His revelations, presented by Radio Free Europe editor Zbigniew Blazynski, were broadcast to Poland by RFE in about two hundred sections and had there the effect of a nuclear bomb. As a result, the Ministry of State Security was liquidated on December 7, 1954, and Romkowski and Fejgin were expelled from the Communist Party and eventually sentenced to fifteen years in jail. The director of the department of investigation at the Ministry, Colonel Joseph Rozanski was arrested at the same time.

6. Colonel Joseph Rozanski (Goldberg), a former clerk in a Warsaw law office and a veteran Communist, was the director of the investigation department of the Ministry of State Security. He handled in 1945 the case of Stefan Korbonski, the former Delegate of the Polish government in exile in London, recognized by the Allied governments. The Delegate—a post held at the time of the Warsaw Rising by Jan Stanislaw Jankowski—was the head of the Polish Underground State, controlling the entire resistance movement and the Home Army. Korbonski and his wife Sophia were arrested in Krakow at night on June 28, 1945.

Rozanski kept them in the building of the Ministry of State Security and did not use torture, which was his favorite method of extorting confessions. He used instead exhausting all night interrogations and threats of summary execution. This relative leniency was no doubt because of the opinion of the supreme authority, Jacob Berman, who said: "Korbonski was the only one in that reactionary gang who tried to save Jews." Charged with abuse of power and extensive use of torture, Rozanski was first sentenced in December 1955 to five years of imprisonment and then to fifteen. He was held in luxuriously appointed quarters and released ten years ahead of time. It was rumored that he settled in Israel.

7. Colonel Czaplicki (fictitious name) who headed the third department of the Ministry of State Security, was charged with the prosecution of the Home Army, the organization of resistance against the Nazis during the war. He was nicknamed "Akower"—a Jewish version of the initials "A.K." of the Home Army. He displayed somewhat less cruelty than the other Bezpieka bosses.

8. Zygmunt Okret was the director of the archives department of the Ministry, in charge of records and personal files.

The above dignitaries were far from being the only Jewish officials of the Ministry. Victor Klosiewicz, a Communist and member of the Council of State, stated in his interview conducted by Teresa Toranska: "Accounts had to be settled in 1955 and it was unfortunate that all the department directors in the Ministry of State Security were Jews."

The reason was Stalin's decision not to use Poles, whom he did not trust, but a more cosmopolitan element. The situation was aptly described by Abel Kainer in his essay *The Jews and Communism*, in the political quarterly *Krytyka*.

The archetype of the Jew during the first ten years of the Polish People's Republic was generally perceived as an agent of the secret political police. It is true that under Bierut and Gomulka (prior to 1948) the key positions in the Ministry of State Security were held by Jews or persons of Jewish background. It is a fact which cannot be overlooked, little known in the west and seldom mentioned by the

Jews in Poland. Both prefer to talk about Stalin's anti-Semitism (the "doctors" plot, etc.). The machine of communist terror functioned in Poland in a matter similar to that used in other communist ruled countries in Europe and elsewhere. What requires explanation is why it is operated by Jews. The reason was that the political police, the base of communist rule, required personnel of unquestionable loyalty to communism. These were people who had joined the Party before the war and in Poland they were predominantly Jewish.

Hence the hierarchy: Stalin in Moscow at the pinnacle, issuing orders to Berman orally during his visits and all-night feasts or by direct telephone line; Berman assigning duties to the directors of the various departments of the Ministry, every one of them Jewish. Since the Ministry of State Security exerted at the time the power of life or death, it held Poland under a reign of terror in the years 1945–1955, at the cost of many lives. Accurate statistics are lacking, but it is well known that thousands perished in prison under torture and maltreatment, for example, the chairman of the Council of National Unity, Kazimierz Puzak. Some were simply executed, such as Wladyslaw Kojder and Narcyz Wiatr, who were commanders of the Peasant Battalions resistance against the Germans. The victims of the reign of terror imposed by Stalin and carried out by his Jewish subordinates during the first ten years after the war numbered tens of thousands. Most of them were Poles who had fought against the Germans in the resistance movement. The Communists judged, quite correctly, that such Poles were the people most likely to oppose the Soviet rule and were therefore to be exterminated. That task was assigned to the Jews because they were thought to be free of Polish patriotism, which was the real enemy.

Other Prominent Jewish Personalities

Aside from leadership in the Ministry of State Security, which played a role analogous to the Gestapo in Hitler's Germany, the

Jews also held leading positions in other government departments of the Communist regime.

Hilary Minc, an economist and a Communist veteran who had spent the years 1939–1944 in Russia and was well known by Stalin, was second in rank only to Jacob Berman. He was the economic dictator and the author of the Three Year Plan. Minc was vice-premier and member of the Politbureau from 1944 to 1956, when he resigned and admitted his "errors and misjudgments."

The third of the group ruling Poland was Roman Zambrowski, born Rubin Nussbaum, who held in turn several dominant political positions. In 1947 he was deputy speaker of the Seym (parliament) and its actual master over the ineffectual speaker Wladyslaw Kowalski. When Stefan Korbonski spoke in the Seym on February 21, 1947, on the subject of a proposed amnesty bill, criticizing sharply the persecution of former members of the resistance against the Germans and demanding a full amnesty for all resistance fighters, the deputy speaker Zambrowski responded with a speech in which he characterized Korbonski's appeal as "an incredible provocation."

Another senior dignitary was Tadeusz Zabludowski, the ruthless director of the Office of the Press, Publications and Entertainments, which was in fact the office of censorship. He banned the publication of parliamentary speeches, such as that of Korbonski regarding the amnesty, and exerted total control over every publication, including books and theater performances as well as films and radio programs. He was assisted by Julia Minc, the wife of Hilary Minc, who headed the Polish News Agency, which was awarded the monopoly in the distribution of news and the management of the press. She was later succeeded by Stanislaw Staszewski, whose family was exterminated in the Holocaust. He was a Communist of long standing.

An important role was also played by Roman Werfl, a Communist since his youth and a talented journalist, who was successively the editor of such periodicals as *Nowe Widnokregi*, *Glos Ludu*, and *Nowe Drogi*. He was the director of the "Ksiazka i Wiedza" publishing house, which enjoyed a monopoly of book publishing. Leon Kasman was the editor of the official Party organ; he had been a Communist already before the war.

One of the dominant figures in the field of publishing and propaganda was Jerzy Borejsza, brother of the secret police colonel Joseph Rozanski, who set the policy of the press and its goals.

He was assisted by "general" Victor Grosz and was promoted during the war in the Soviet Union from enlisted man to general for political services. He was the head of the political education department of the Polish army and was charged with the Communist indoctrination of the troops.

An important role was also played by Eugeniusz Szyr, a veteran of the Spanish civil war and a member of the "Union of Polish Patriots" formed in Moscow. He held the office of vice-premier.

Key positions in the Communist Party were held by Arthur Starewicz, secretary of the central committee of the Party, also a member of the Union of Polish Patriots, generally known as "The Muscovites."

A different role was assigned to Adam Schaff, a prewar Communist and a scholar and professor. He dedicated himself to the spreading of Marxist philosophy and published numerous works on the subject.

The Jews in the Ministry of Foreign Affairs

The key positions in the Ministry of Foreign Affairs were held by Jews, often with assumed Polish names. Wincenty Rzymowski, a Pole, served as front man, with the title of minister, but the actual control was in the hands of vice-minister Zygmunt Modzelewski. The office of the ostensible minister of foreign affairs was later held by such insignificant figures as Stanislaw Skrzeszewski, who was a school teacher in Krakow before the war, as well as others, including Stefan Werblowski, greeted at the airport on his return from abroad by a delegation of Jewish officials, Marian Naszkowski and others. The control of the ministry was in the hands of Mieczyslaw Ogrodzinski, who adopted a Polish name as did his colleagues.

An important diplomatic role was played by Julius Katz-Suchy, Poland's delegate to the United Nations, and Manfred Lachs, who served as chairman of the legal committee of the UN Assembly and was later appointed a member of the International Tribunal in The Hague. There were many ambassadors and consuls, among them Henryk Strasburger and Waclaw Szymanowski; Consul Tadeusz Kassern, who became disenchanted with the system and committed suicide; Eugene Milnikiel, ambassador in London; Ludwik Rajchman, head of a Polish economic mission to the United States, and many others.

In addition to the key personalities mentioned here, a very heavy proportion of the senior and middle-level officials were also Jewish.

The Jews in the Ministry of Justice

Henryk Swiatkowski, a Christian Pole, served as the figurehead with the title of minister. The Ministry of Justice was actually under the control of Leon Szajn, the vice-minister, prewar president of the leftist Association of Legal Aides and wartime member of the Union of Polish Patriots sponsored by Stalin in Moscow. After the war he was assigned to the Democratic Party, kept by the Communists to ensure appearances of pluralism for the benefit of the West. He soon became the secretary general of that party, as well as vice-minister of justice. His principal assistants were Stefan Rozmaryn and the prosecutor Jacob Sawicki, together with Colonel Stefan Kurowski, who represented Poland at the Nuremberg trials of the Nazi leaders. All of the above were Jewish. When Sawicki wanted to send to Nuremberg Stefan Korbonski as witness, Kurowski refused to allow him to testify personally. Korbonski's testimony, concerning mainly the·mass street executions, was presented by the Soviet prosecutor Smirnov and figures in volume 7 of the "Trial of the major war criminals before the International Military

Tribunal." The German governor Frank was sentenced to death and hanged. Stefan Kurowski ended his career as the chief justice of the Supreme Court, which counted several Jewish judges, among them Mieczyslaw Szerer.

The leader of the defense counsels was attorney Maslanko, the dean of a team of political defenders whose only function was to induce suspects to confess to real or fictitious crimes, after which the defenders confined themselves to asking for lenient sentences. The Ministry of State Security—Bezpieka, the Polish equivalent of the KGB—expected the lawyers to help the prosecution, not to defend the accused. The director of the investigation department, Rozanski, made it clear that a defense counsel's duty was to collect evidence against the accused. Judges, eager to stay on the right side of the secret political police, would call Rozanski to ask him what sentence he would suggest for a person charged by his office. Rozanski replies were laconic: "five years . . . ten years . . . life . . . death."

The Jews in Parliament and the Political Elite

The Jewish contingent in the Seym was headed by the vice-speaker Zambrowski, mentioned earlier. He was assisted by Boleslaw Drobner, a prewar member of the Polish Socialist Party, which was not pro-Communist. Asked in the parliamentary lobby by his old friend Mikolajczyk how he managed to get on the Communist bench, Drobner replied: "I did time in a Soviet jail and I don't want to do so again." Other Jewish members of the prewar Socialist Party who joined the Communists were Dorota Kluszynska, Alfred Krygier, and Julian Hochfeld, an eager convert.

Among other members of the ruling Jewish–Communist elite were: Stefan Zolkiewski, minister of education in the years 1956–1959, who made Communist indoctrination the first priority; Ludwik Grosfeld, former minister of finance of the government in exile, who after his return to Poland joined the

Communist National Council; Emil Sommerstein, a prewar member of parliament, appointed minister for war reparations; the eminent poet Julian Tuwim, who returned to Poland from the West in 1946 to become an enthusiastic champion of Communist rule; Wladyslaw Matwin, one of the founding members of the Moscow Union of Polish Patriots, who held several important positions, among them that of editor of the chief Communist press organ, the *Trybuna Ludua* (Tribune of the People); Anthony Alster, vice-minister of the Interior; Stefan Arski, well-known journalist and senior official of the Communist Party; Isaac Kleinerman, head of the office of the presidium of the National Council; Jacob Prawin, Party activist; and Ozias Szechter, a veteran Communist.

The major part of that leadership group of Jewish prominence came to Poland from Russia, where it had fled during the war. It exerted totalitarian rule over Poland from 1945 to about 1955 and the "Polish October" of 1956. To ensure its control of the country, it jailed the leading non-Jewish Polish Communists, such as Wladyslaw Gomulka, Zenon Kliszka, Marian Spychalski, General Gregory Korczynski, General Waclaw Komar, and Marshal Michal Zymirski, and many others.

The October events of 1956 resulted in a change of guard, when the non-Jewish Communists such as Gomulka seized power and sent to jail Roman Romkowski, Anatol Fejgin, and Joseph Rozanski, as well as many of their associates.

The Jewish elite which played a dominant role in the Communist rule of postwar Poland found its epilogue in the exodus of 1967–1968. The Kracow *Tygodnik Powszechny* published in its issue of March 20, 1988, excerpts from an article in the Communist periodical *Nowe Drogi* that describe the events of March 1968:

> Between the second half of 1967 and that of 1968 341 officers of Jewish origin were dismissed from the army. They were also ousted from the communist party. . . . In Warsaw, 483 persons were removed from senior official positions, 365 of them from the ministries and central agencies, 49 from academic posts and 24 from the press and cultural institutions. . . . Six ministers and vice-ministers were

removed from office, 35 directors and department heads . . . about 70 professors and lecturers . . . by mid 1969 over 20,000 Jews emigrated from Poland.

The cause of that exodus was found far away from Poland. It was the overwhelming victory of the Israeli army in the six–day war with Egypt and other Arabic neighbors. It was greeted in Poland with joy and loud cries of "Our Jews smashed the Soviet Arabs!" That reaction was reported to the highest levels of the Kremlin, not by the silent Soviet Jews, but by the Polish ones, which was enough to cause their expulsion. In contrast, the Soviet Jews were kept in Russia as hostages of the West. That is how the events were interpreted in Poland.

In the United States and western Europe the departure of the Jewish Communist dignitaries from Poland was met with a storm of protests, among them that of a thousand American professors. Stefan Korbonski commented on them in a letter published on July 13, 1968, in the *New York Times:*

To the Editor:
The well justified protest of 1,000 professors against the present anti-Semitic purge in Poland (advertisement July 2) does not pay sufficient attention to the fact that the Polish people are not taking any part in this purge which is occurring inside the Communist Party, since the prevailing majority of the purged people are its prominent members.
The Polish people, who do not have any say in this matter or others, consider it purely a family affair of the present "owners of Poland." And, if nobody sheds tears at the dismissal of such dominant figures of the Stalinist period as Roman Zambrowski, Stefan Zolkiewski, Juliusz Katz-Suchy, Stefan Staszewski and Prof. Adam Schaff, it is not because they are Jews, but because they are Communists rejected by the Polish people in the same way as Gomulka and his clique, or General Moczar and his secret police.

Stefan Korbonski
Washington, July 2, 1968

The writer was a member of the Polish Parliament in 1947, representing the anti-Communist Polish Peasant Party.

The ten years of Jewish rule in Poland could not be easily forgotten. It was an era of the midnight knock at the door, arbitrary arrests, torture, and sometimes secret execution. Most of those responsible for that reign of terror left Poland and upon arrival in the West represented themselves as victims of Communism and anti-Semitism—a claim which was readily believed in the West and earned them the full support of their hosts.

CHAPTER VI

The Jews Abroad

The American Jews

THE HOLOCAUST SAW THE EXTERMINATION OF OVER THREE MIL-lion Jews in Poland; they had constituted about 10 percent of the population and were more numerous than the citizens of the state of Israel when it was estabished in 1948. After the Holocaust, the United States became the home of the largest concentration of Jews in the world. New York City alone has about three million Jewish residents, about the same number that Poland had before the war.

In Poland the Jews were divided into two groups: those who considered themselves Poles of Jewish faith and spoke Polish and those who, while Polish citizens under the law, did not identify with Polish nationality and spoke mostly Yiddish. There is no such division in the United States, where all Jews are

Americans of Jewish faith and very few speak Yiddish. Only a few individuals, such as Rabbi Kahane, regard themselves as Israelites with American citizenship.

While in Poland only a minority of the Jews joined the mainstream of national life and the majority lived in self-created ghettos and "stetls," in the United States the overwhelming majority participate actively in national life and even attain dominant positions in such areas as finance, the media, entertainment, law, medicine, and learning. A large proportion of the 191 Nobel prizes awarded to Americans have been won by Jews. Names such as Bernard Baruch, adviser to presidents; Albert Einstein; Admiral Hyman Rickover, the Polish-born father of the nuclear submarine; Senator Jacob Javits, and countless others are examples of the role played by the Jews in the United States. American freedom has provided an ideal climate for the development of the talents of the Jews.

A unique relationship has been established between the United States and the state of Israel, sometimes described as the fifty-first state, financed and supported by the other fifty states. The American Jews, more numerous than the citizens of Israel, promote the interests of their brothers. The principal instrument of such support is the Jewish Lobby, whose activities are described in the *New York Times* of July 6, 1987:

> After several decades of growth in size and sophistication, the leading pro-Israel lobby in Washington, the American Israel Public Affairs Committee, has become a major force in shaping United States policy in the Middle East.
>
> Operating from tightly guarded offices just north of the Capitol, the organization has gained the power to influence a Presidential candidate's choice of staff, to block practically any arms sale to an Arab country and to serve as a catalyst for intimate military relations between the Pentagon and the Israeli Army. Its leading officials are consulted by State Department and White House policy makers, by Senators and generals.
>
> The committee, known by its acronym Aipac, is an American lobby, not an Israeli one—it says its funds come from individual Americans—and it draws on a broad sympathy for the cause of Israel in the Administration, Congress and the American public. As a result, it has become the envy of competing lobbyists and the bane of

Middle East specialists who would like to strengthen ties with pro-Western Arabs.

"It tends to skew the consideration of issues," a senior State Department official said. "People don't look very hard at some options." This narrows the Administration's internal policy discussions, he said, precluding even the serious study of ideas known to be anathema to Aipac, such as the sale of some advanced weapons systems to Saudi Arabia or Jordan.

A former official in the Reagan White House gave a different assessment. While Aipac is "a factor, nothing was ever excluded as an option for consideration," he said, "I know of no case where it was decisive, at least in the analytical phase." The greater influence seemed to be at the political, decision-making level, he said.

Aipac is already gearing up for the 1988 Presidential campaign. So impressive is its political mystique that now, 16 months before the 1988 elections, nearly all the Presidential candidates have already met with Aipac officials to be interviewed about their positions on the Middle East. . . .

After the Holocaust, the American Jews adopted a two-pronged policy. On the one hand, they endeavored to avoid an excessive immigration of Jews to America, which might contribute to anti-Semitism. That is why Israel was generously funded so that it could receive the survivors of the Holocaust. On the other hand, those Jews who managed to enter the United States were offered the fullest assistance; for example, by granting them substantial credits for establishing a business. No other immigrant group enjoys such support.

The Two Jewish Theories

A surprise awaited Jews arriving in the United States from Poland. They were astounded by the hatred of Poland by the American Jews, a hatred which was manifested in a variety of ways. As time dimmed the memory of what actually happened during the war, a version blaming the Poles for the Holocaust almost to the same extent as the Nazis began to gain currency among the American Jews. They charged the Poles with indifference and even collusion with the Germans. Any Jew arriving from Poland who dared to contradict that theory was soon silenced and denied any assistance if he persevered. Though knowing the charges to be untrue, the new arrivals could hardly contradict their benefactors for fear of losing their support. The Polish Americans, at least as numerous as the Jews but not as influential, were deeply hurt by such unfounded accusations. The Poles arriving from Communist-ruled Poland were also astounded by the hostility which greeted them from the American Jews.

The second theory propagated by the American Jews asserts that anyone who disagrees with a Jew on any point of fact or opinion is an anti-Semite. Consequently, the Poles in general and those in America in particular are charged first with being somehow co-responsible for the Holocaust and then with denying it.

Several books published in the United States, such as *The Samaritans* and *Righteous Among Nations* by Wladyslaw Bartoszewski, *He Who Saves One Life* by Iranek Osmecki, *Poland in the Second World War* by Joseph Garlinski, *The Polish Underground State* by Stefan Korbonski, and many others were ignored by the American media because they presented the truth about the events in Poland during the war.

Some attacks against the Poles appeared in the press, such as that of Joseph Brandes of Paterson State College, Wayne, New Jersey, in the *New York Times* of April 26, 1963. It met with a response by Stefan Korbonski, the last chief of the Polish underground government, who wrote in the *New York Times* of May 9, 1963:

> The letter of Joseph Brandes published April 26 is unfair to the Polish people, who—contrary to Mr. Brandes' claims—tried very hard to help the Jews within the Warsaw ghetto walls, although the Poles risked death by extending any kind of help. An eyewitness who cannot be suspected of being partial to Poles, the late Prof. Philip Friedman, dean of the Jewish Teachers Seminary in New York, writes about such aid in his two books: "Their Brothers' Keepers" and "Martyrs and Fighters."
>
> Professor Friedman describes aid given to the Jews by all strata of the Polish population—including pre-war anti-Semites and Catholic

clergy and nuns—who hid 20,000 Jews in Warsaw and its suburbs alone, supplied them with Arayan documents, and smuggled food into the ghetto. The Polish underground alerted Western allies to the fate of the Jews with the aid of clandestine radio transmitters, and established the Committee to Help Jews with two Jewish members, Leon Feiner and Adolf Berman. The committee succeeded in saving 4,000 Jewish people.

The underground also issued proclamations protesting mass murder, helped to buy arms, which at that time were priceless, delivered some—although few—weapons to the Warsaw ghetto fighters, and prepared for them escape routes through the city sewers.

May I add that some Polish hoodlums who cooperated with the Nazis in persecuting the Jews were sentenced to death by the underground courts and executed. Their names and the place and date of the executions were published in the underground press.

During the ghetto uprising the Polish underground Home Army launched several diversionary attacks against German troops who encircled the ghetto, in places and at times pre-arranged with ghetto fighters, enabling the Jews to escape.

One year later, on Aug. 1, 1944, the Warsaw uprising broke out with only one fighter out of every four armed. It resulted in the death of 200,000 people and the total destruction of the city of Warsaw. Both uprisings met a similar fate, so the continuation of recrimination does not make much sense.

Life magazine carried on January 22, 1965, a photograph of a "Jewish feather peddler about to be shipped to the Polish gas chambers." Korbonski responded in a letter published in *Life's* issue of February 12, 1965:

Sirs:
 "Incident at Vichy" (Jan. 22) shows a picture of the Jewish feather peddler who is to "be shipped to the Polish gas chambers."
 This caption is misleading. There were no "Polish" gas chambers, only Nazi gas chambers in Poland, where along with Jews thousands of Poles were gassed.

The *Washington Post* published on August 8, 1967, an article about frictions within the Polish Communist Party, triggered by the Israel problem. Korbonski replied in his letter of August 13:

In connection with the report, "Israeli Issue Creates Polish Party Tension" published in *The Washington Post* of Aug. 8, I should like to emphasize that the Polish people were outraged by the anti-Israeli campaign launched by Wladyslaw Gomulka. The true feelings of the Polish people were expressed by Cardinal Stefan Wyszynski who, after his sermon delivered in Warsaw on June 5, prayed for Israel. Also General Wladyslaw Anders sent a letter from London to General Moshe Dayan congratulating him on behalf of the Poles abroad on a brilliant victory. In his acknowledgment, General Dayan expressed the hope that victory would be followed by political success.

Raymond H. Anderson referred in his article in the *New York Times* of April 20, 1973, to the aid given by the Polish Home Army to the Jewish fighters in the ghetto. Korbonski contributed additional information on the subject in his letter published May 7, 1973:

> As last head of the Polish wartime underground, there is an addendum I would like to make to the news article of April 20 by Raymond H. Anderson "Warsaw, April 19, 1943: The Ghetto Battle Is On."
>
> Among other things, this article spoke of the aid given to the Jewish combat organization by the Polish Underground Home Army. From our own very meagre supplies we delivered to it the following quantities of weapons and ammunition: two machine guns; seventy revolvers, all with magazines and ammunition; ten rifles; 600 hand grenades with detonators; 66 pounds of plastic explosives received via parachute drops; 400 detonators for bombs and grenades; 66 pounds of potassium for Molotov cocktails; and large quantities of nitric acid, necessary for the production of gunpowder.
>
> During the Ghetto uprising, Home Army commandos attacked German sentries posted at the Ghetto gates, and tried to breach the Ghetto walls with mines to open a way of escape for the fighting Jews. Unfortunately, our commando attacks were repulsed, and two demolition experts were killed and a third was wounded.
>
> The heroic stand by the Jews of the Warsaw Ghetto in the face of overwhelming odds won the admiration of the entire Polish resistance movement. We join in saluting the memory of all those who died in this historic battle.

Responding to inaccurate information about Menachem Begin, then prime minister of Israel, in the July 21, 1977, issue of the *Washington Star,* Korbonski wrote a letter published in that newspaper on August 8, 1977:

> In connection with the letters on "The Past of Begin" (July 21), I would like to add that Mr. Begin, born and educated in Poland, also received there his basic military and underground training, the latter based upon the experiences of the Polish conspiracies which had organized the anti-Russian uprisings of 1831, 1863, the revolution of 1905 and, finally the Pilsudski Legions in 1914.
>
> The Polish pre-war government supported the policy of the Zionist-Revisionist Movement and its military arm, Irgun Zvai Leumi, aimed at the creation of an independent Jewish state. The head of the movement, Vladimir Jabotinsky, Mr. Begin's mentor and teacher, was supported financially by this government, which established paramilitary training camps for Irgun in Poland and also supplied Irgun with arms smuggled to Palestine by way of Romania and Bulgaria.
>
> After the outbreak of the German-Russo war in 1941, Mr. Begin, having been released from the Soviet concentration camp, volunteered for the Polish army organized by Gen. Wladyslaw Anders on Soviet territory, and came with this army to Palestine in 1942.
>
> Contrary to the widely spread rumors, he did not desert this army. I quote Mr. Begin, himself, on the subject.
>
> "The army whose uniform I wear and to which I swore my allegiance fights with the mortal enemy of the Jewish nation, the Nazi Germany. One can not desert from such an army even to fight for the freedom of one's own fatherland".
>
> In fact Mr. Begin was honorably discharged from the Polish army and joined Irgun Zvai Leumi, which turned out to be a steppingstone to his present position as prime minister.

Young ambitious Jews arriving from Poland soon realized that the acceptance of both theories was to their personal advantage. One of them was Jan Tomasz Gross, who, in his book *The Polish Society Under German Occupation,* attacked the Delegate of the government in exile Stanislaw Jankowski and the command of the Home Army, charging them with anti-Semitism. Yet he knew very well that many Jews fought in the ranks of the Home Army, including several officers at its headquarters. Stefan Korbonski responded to that unfounded accusation in his review of Gross's book in the *Zeszyty Historyczne* publication.

Abraham Brumberg continued in similar vein when he al-

leged in the *New York Times Book Review* of October 19, 1986, and
in *Tikkun* for July-August 1987 that the Home Army was anti-
Semitic and did not enlist Jews. Stefan Korbonski replied in the
article "When Did Edelman Tell the Truth?" in the *New York
Polish Daily* of December 18, 1986.

When Did Edelman Tell the Truth?

Abraham Brumberg's review of Hanna Krall's book *Shielding
the Flame*, in the *New York Times Book Review* of October 19, 1986,
commented on her account of the life of Mark Edelman, who
was the second in command of Mordecai Anielewicz, the
leader of the Warsaw rising of 1943.

Brumberg starts by saying that the ghetto rising restored the
honor of the Jews in the eyes of the romantic Poles. He then
steps outside the book under review and asserts as his own
opinion that Edelman did not tell Hanna Krall the truth when
she interviewed him in 1976. According to Brumberg, Edelman
revealed the truth only in an interview with the underground
newspaper *Czas* in 1985, when he said that the Jewish ghetto
fighters did not get any weapons from the Polish Home Army,
which did not enlist Jews and was so anti-Semitic that after the
liquidation of the ghetto Edelman was afraid to ask for its help,
suspecting that they might kill him.

Astounded by these allegations, I secured a copy of Hanna
Krall's *Shielding the Flame*. Brumberg simply ignored the author's
statements, substituting his own. Edelman had told Hanna Krall
that the Jewish freedom fighter Michael Klepfisz was
posthumously decorated by General Sikorski with the Virtuti
Militari cross. He also told her that he conferred with the Polish
underground parties and never encountered any discourtesy in
dealings outside the ghetto with the Polish underground.
Edelman also said that the Jewish fighters received sixty fire-
arms from the Home Army and the Polish Workers' Party, and
that during the ghetto rising a Polish unit carried out an attack at

Franciszkanska Street to divert the Germans. He added that he had himself fought in the ranks of the Home Army in its rising of 1944, that he wore a red and white armband, that after the rising the men of the Home Army helped the escape of the Jews, that there was a Polish Council for Help to the Jews called "Zegota," that the Jews received dollars from air drops for the Home Army, and that the Jewish Fighting Organization placed itself under the orders of General Grot-Rowecki. Grot-Rowecki assigned Chrusciel (war name Monter) as his deputy colonel and Zbigniew Lewandowski as military instructor, and also provided weapons. Edelman also stated that the female Catholic convents gave shelter to the Jews and sometimes stored weapons and explosives for them, that the Polish red and white standard was flown in the ghetto during the rising alongside the Jewish blue and white—a fact which deeply moved the Polish population, which regarded Edelman as a hero.

I was particularly glad to encounter in Hanna Krall's book the name of Henryk Wolinski, frequently referred to by Edelman in most cordial terms. I knew him from prewar days when we were both lawyers. During the war and the occupation he became an officer at the headquarters of the Home Army and was assigned the department of Jewish affairs.

In July 1942 I was instructed to contact a person who could pass on to me information obtained by secret channels from the ghetto. I was eager to secure such intelligence and looked forward to the meeting. To my surprise the mysterious Kowalewski, who was to be my contact, turned out to be my old friend Wolinski. He started to supply me with information which I then condensed for transmitting by radio to the Polish government in London. Here is a sample message:

> June 20, 1944. Massive extermination started on May 15, in Auschwitz. The Jews go first, then the Soviet prisoners of war and the so-called "sick." Large transports of Hungarian Jews are coming in. Thirteen trains a day, each with 40 to 50 cars. The victims are convinced that they are due for a prisoners' exchange or resettlement. The gas chambers are operating nonstop. Corpses are burnt in crematoria or in the open. At least 100,000 have been gassed.

After the war I lost touch with Wolinski, but he later established contact with me in Washington. He was practicing law in Katowice in Poland, and we maintained correspondence until his death in 1986. The Warsaw newspaper *Zycie Warszawy* published two obituary notices: the first, from his family, mentioned the fact that Wolinski was awarded by Israel the Yad Vashem medal for Gentiles who saved Jews; the second, signed by Mark Edelman, conveyed homage to Wolinski "on behalf of all the soldiers of the Jewish Fighting Organization."

It is obvious that Mark Edelman made the statements reported by Hanna Krall in her book and confirmed by his recent message on Wolinski's death. The statements ascribed by Brumberg to Edelman were probably never made by him and are at any rate totally untrue.

The allegation that the Home Army refused to enlist Jews is a lie. Even at the Home Army headquarters, in its general staff there were several officers of Jewish origin, among them Marceli Handelsman, Ludwik Widerszal, and Jerzy Makowiecki, to mention a few. There was no restriction at all even at the higher levels of command, much less for the rank and file.

Did Mark Edelman really tell one story to Hanna Krall in 1976 and its opposite to Brumberg in 1985? I am awaiting his explanation.

Along with attacks against the Polish underground resistance and its Home Army, a campaign glorifying the Jews in the ghetto was unleashed. Lucy Dawidowicz wrote regarding the ghetto rising which broke out in Warsaw on April 19, 1943, that the first shots fired at the Germans in occupied Europe were those of the ghetto fighters. Yet the Polish forests were swarming with partisans since 1939. They attacked German convoys, blew up railroad bridges, and took on small German garrisons. At the same time General Mihailovich's partisans were fighting in Yugoslavia, as were the Communists and the Maquis who operated in parts of France.

Dawidowicz's claim to the effect that the Warsaw Jews were in 1943 the first to fight the Germans in occupied Europe is so absurd as to cast much doubt on the accuracy of her other statements.

The Messenger from Poland

On October 26, 1981, the conference hall at the State Department was in a state of unusual animation. Several hundred people were attending a conference organized by the United States Holocaust Memorial Council and presided over by Elie Wiesel. The purpose of the conference was a meeting between the former prisoners and their liberators in order to, as Wiesel put it, "bear witness to what we have seen and done." It was funded by a businessman, William B. Konar, who survived the Holocaust and the Nazi concentration camps as a boy and was now hugging the retired American general Francis B. Roberts, who—then a captain in the 95th infantry division—was the first to enter the camp of Niederhagen and liberate its inmates. Deeply moved by the memory, the two men recalled aloud their meeting of many years ago.

The hall was gradually filling with the delegations of the liberating nations, among them the Soviet and Polish ones. The son of a prisoner, Abraham J. Peck, was also embracing the Soviet general Alexey Gorlinski and thanking him for setting his father free from the camp of Teresin. Earlier a former prisoner of Buchenwald had to leave the hall sobbing when a former captain of Canadian artillery described the single great moan with which the prisoners greeted his entry to the camp of Westbork. Everyone was moved by the couple, Gerda and Kurt Klein. She was a concentration camp inmate and he an American soldier who set her free and then married her.

The principal speaker was Jan Karski, now professor at Georgetown University, then a secret emissary of the Polish government in exile, who penetrated some camps at the risk of his life in order to bring back to the West an eyewitness report. He managed to do so and presented to British and American leaders, including Franklin D. Roosevelt, a detailed report on the tragedy then in progress. Now he described his mission, and Representative Stephen Solarz (D., NY) was so impressed by the account that he included it in its entirety in the *Congressional Record* of December 15, 1981:

Mr. Speaker, recently a significant and deeply moving conference was held at the State Department. Organized by the U.S. Holocaust Memorial Council and chaired by the Honorable Elie Wiesel, the International Liberators Conference, October 26–28, was to commemorate the suffering and sacrifice of those who perished in the Nazi concentration camps during World War II, and the liberation of those who survived. In the words of President Reagan the Conference served "as a stark reminder to the world's conscience of what transpired during that period of history and will strengthen our resolve to prevent mankind from sinking into that ultimate horror again."

Conference participants came from many lands, including both those who liberated the camps, and those victims of the Nazi terror who still lived. I had the opportunity to attend the Conference and I shall not try to relate here my own reactions. Suffice it to say that the Conference was unique in my experience.

However, I do wish to call to the attention of my colleagues one exceptionally important speech which was delivered at the Conference. The subject under discussion was: "Discovering the 'Final Solution'." In other words, when did the Free World first find out about Nazi plans and actions designed to exterminate the Jews? Was it only after the war had ended, when Allied troops liberated the concentration camps? Or had it been possible for those suffering under Nazi oppression to send out word of the Holocaust even while the war was under way? And if the free world leaders learned of the Holocaust during the war, what action did they take? One speaker was uniquely qualified to answer that question, Dr. Jan Karski, a hero of the Polish underground, a secret emissary to the West, and today a professor at Georgetown University.

Dr. Karski was born in Poland. He entered the diplomatic service of his country, was mobilized in 1939, was taken prisoner by the Soviet Army. He escaped shortly thereafter, and joined the Polish anti-Nazi underground in German-occupied Poland. As an underground courier he made several secret trips to France, Great Britain, and America during the war. During these highly dangerous trips Dr. Karski carried messages and appeals not only from the Polish underground leadership, but also from two Jewish organizations, the Bund and the Zionists. He was authorized to speak for all those groups.

True to that trust he conveyed the desperate appeals and hopes of those he represented. He made clear the plight of the Jews, the terrible dangers which threatened them, and their specific recommendations for free world action on their behalf. Dr. Karski's report reveals some responded favorably to these appeals, and others, to their shame, did not. I will let Dr. Karski's words speak for themselves on that subject. But one thing comes through very clearly: by 1943 free world leaders had been informed of the Holocaust. They knew.

Mr. Speaker, I ask that Dr. Karski's address at the Liberators Conference be included in today's CONGRESSIONAL RECORD.

INTERNATIONAL LIBERATORS CONFERENCE, 1981

The subject "Discovering the 'Final Solution' " requires consideration of the following questions:

What and when did the Western leaders as well as the Western public opinion learn about the Holocaust?

In what way did the information reach them?

What was the reaction? According to evidence?

I, among many, did play a part in this story. In preparing my report I had in mind not only our Conference but historical record, as well.

In the middle of the Summer 1942 I received a message from the Delegate of the Polish government in exile for the Homeland, Cyril Ratajski, that he approved of my request to be sent secretly to London as a courier for the leaders of political parties organized in the Central Political Committee, and for the Delegate himself. The coming expedition was to be my fourth secret trip between Warsaw-Paris-London.

Sometime in September 1942, the Delegate informed me that the leaders of two Jewish underground organizations: the Socialist Bund and the Zionists learned about my mission and requested permission to use my services for their own communications to their representatives in London; to the Polish government and to the Allied authorities. The Delegate was sympathetic and I agreed.

Soon after, I met the two Jewish leaders on two occasions. They met me jointly to emphasize that their communications were in behalf of all Polish Jews regardless of their political differences. They identified themselves by their functions (naturally, no names). All post-war literature identifies them as Leon Feiner, (Bund leader) and Adolf Berman (Zionist). For the record I must add, that an Israeli scholar, Walter Laqueur, in his recently published book, "The Terrible Secret," suggests that the Zionist leader might have been Menahem Kirschenbaum.

The Jewish leaders sent through me various messages, instructions and appeals to various quarters. I selected only those which directly pertain to the subject under discussion. Some other, important ones, I shall regretfully, ignore.

MY MISSION TO THE POLISH AND ALLIED GOVERNMENTS

The unprecedented destruction of the entire Jewish population is not motivated by Germany's military requirements. Hitler and his subordinates aim at the total destruction of the Jews before the war ends and regardless of its outcome. The Polish and Allied governments cannot disregard this reality. The Jews in Poland are helpless. They have no country of their own. They have no independent voice in the Allied councils. They cannot rely on the Polish Underground or population-at-large. They might save some individuals—they are unable to stop the extermination. Only the powerful Allied governments can help effectively.

The Polish Jews appeal to the Polish and Allied Governments to undertake measures in an attempt to stop the extermination.

They place historical responsibility on the Polish and Allied governments if they fail to undertake those measures.

This is what the Jews demand:

A public announcement that prevention of the physical extermination of the Jews become a part of the over-all Allied war strategy.

Informing the German nation through radio, air-dropped leaflets and other means about their government's crimes committed against the Jews. All available data on the Jewish ghettos; concentration and extermination camps; names of the German officials directly involved in the crimes; statistics; facts; methods used should be spelled-out;

Public and formal demand for evidence that such a pressure had been exercised and Nazi practices directed against the Jews stopped;

Placing the responsibility on the German nation as a whole if they failed to respond and if the extermination continues;

Public and formal announcement that in view of the unprecedented Nazi crimes against the Jews and in hope that those crimes would stop, the Allied governments were to take unprecedented steps: Certain areas and objects in Germany would be bombed in retaliation. German people would be informed before and after each action that the Nazi continued extermination of the Jews prompted the bombing.

Jewish leaders in London, particularly Szmul Zygelbojm (Bund) and Dr. Ignace Szwarcbard (Zionist), are solemnly charged to make all efforts so as to make the Polish government formally forward these demands at the Allied councils.

TO THE PRESIDENT OF THE POLISH REPUBLIC, WLADYSLAW RACZKIEWICZ

Many among those who directly or indirectly contribute to the Jewish tragedy profess their Catholic faith. The Polish and other European Jews sent to Poland feel entitled on humanitarian and spiritual grounds to expect protection of the Vatican. Religious sanctions, excommunication included, are within the Pope's jurisdiction. Such sanctions, publically proclaimed might have an impact on the German people. They might even make Hitler, a baptized Catholic, to reflect.

Because the nature of this message and the source it came from as well as because of diplomatic protocal's requirements, I was instructed to deliver the message to the President of the Republic only. Let him use his conscience and wisdom in approaching the Pope. I was explicitly forbidden to discuss that subject with the Jewish leaders. Their possible maladroit intervention might be counterproductive.

TO THE PRIME MINISTER AND COMMANDER IN CHIEF. GENERAL WLADYSLAW SIKORSKI, MINISTER OF INTERIOR, STANISLAW MIKOLAJCZYK, ZYGELBOJM AND SZWARCBARD

Although the Polish people at large sympathize or try to help the Jews, many criminals blackmail, rob, denounce or murder the Jews in hiding. The Underground authorities must apply punitive sanctions against them, executions included. In the last case, the identity of the guilty ones and the nature of their crimes should be publicized in the Underground press.

Zygelbojm and Szwarcbard must use all their pressure, so that pertinent instructions would be issued.

In order to avoid any risk of anti-Polish propaganda, I was explicitly forbidden to discuss that subject with non-Polish Jewish leaders. I was to inform Zygelbojm and Szwarcbard about that part of my instructions.

TO THE ALLIED INDIVIDUAL GOVERNMENT/CIVIC LEADERS AS WELL AS TO INTERNATIONAL JEWISH LEADERS

There is a possiblity to save some Jews if money were available. Gestapo is corrupted not only on the low level but also on the medium and even high level. They would cooperate for gold or hard currency. The Jewish leaders are able to make appropriate contacts.

Some Jews would be allowed to leave Poland provided they have original foreign passports. Origins of those passports are unimportant. As large supply of such passports as possible should be sent. They must be blank. Forged names, identification data, etc., would be overlooked by the German authorities—for money, or course;

Provisions must be made that those Jews who do succeed in leaving Poland would be accepted in the Allied or neutral countries;

Some Jews of not semitic appearance could leave the ghettos, obtain false German documents and live among other Poles under assumed names. Money to bribe the ghetto's guards, various officials like (Arbeitsamt) is needed.

Money, medicines, food, clothing are most urgently needed by the survivors in the ghettos. Subsidies obtained from the Delegate of the Polish government as well as other funds sent through various channels by the Jewish international organizations are totally insufficient. More hard currency, sent without any delay, is a question of life or death for thousands of Jews.

In addition to all the messages I was to carry, both Jewish leaders solemnly committed me to do my utmost in arousing the public opinion in the free world on behalf of the Jews. I solemnly swore, that should I arrive safely in London, I would not fail them.

At the end of the second meeting, the Bund leader confronted me with the following. He knows the English people. My report might seem incredible. My mission would be enhanced if I were able to say that I witnessed the Jewish tragedy. The Jewish Underground does have some contacts, even with Gestapo. They are able to smuggle me to the Warsaw ghetto. They are even able to smuggle me—in disguise—to the Belsec camp. In the ghetto, he himself, would be my guide. In Belsec—a Nazi official would take care of my expedition. Both trips are dangerous—but they are feasible. He has no right to ask me to undertake them. But, "Withold" (my psuedonym at the time) "I know much about you and your work. Would you volunteer to help our Jewish cause?" I agreed.

I visited the Jewish ghetto twice, in the middle of October 1942. A few days later, I visited Belsec—all three trips proved successful. These trips became the last items in collecting data, messages, instructions, complaints of various political leaders in the Underground. Two or three days later, I embarked on my secret journey to London.

Again my trip was successful. It lasted 21 days: Warsaw-Berlin-Brussels-Paris-Lyon-Perpignan-Pyrenees Mountains on foot-Barcelona-Madrid-Algeciras-Gibraltar. A ceremonial dinner with the Governor. A good night sleep. A plane was waiting. In last week of November, 1942, I already began reporting in London. Of course, one must realize that my Jewish reports were only a part of my overall mission. In addition, I was supposed to go back to Poland—on my fifth mission. The Polish Prime Minister's office which organized all of my contacts asked every individual I had been sent to not to identify me publicly.

As to my Jewish materials, I was not ihe only informant. Since 1941, secret radio contacts with London functioned. Coded data on the Jewish ghetto's deportations, extermination had been regularly transmitted from Poland to London for information and public distribution. Most of the messages, however, were considered as lacking credibility. The head of the secret radio service, throughout the entire war, was Stefan Korbonski eventually, the last head of the Polish Underground State.

The most important personalities in England to whom I made reports on the Jewish situation (November 1942–June 1943):

(1) The Poles

All government and political leaders: Liaison to Cardinal Hlond (at the time residing in the Vatican); Mgr. Kaczynski; Jewish leaders: Zygelbojm (Bund); Szwarcbard (Zionists); Grosfeld (Socialist).

(2) The English: Four members of the War Cabinet

Anthony Eden, Foreign Secretary; Arthur Greenwood, Labor Party; Lord Cranborne, Conservative Party; Hugh Dalton, President of the Board of Trade. Then: Lord Selbourne, War Office, European underground resistance: Miss Ellen Wilkinson, Labor, Member of Parliment; William Henderson, Labor Party leader, Member of Parliament; Owen O'Malley, British ambassador to the Polish government; Anthony D. Biddle, American ambassador to the Polish government.

United Nations War Crime Commission, Sir Cecil Hurst, chairman.

I pressed for and did contact several non-government personalities:

H. G. Welles, world-known author; Arthur Koestler, world-known author; Victor Gollancz, publishing firm of his name; Allen Lane, publishing firm Penguine; Kingsley Martin, editor-in-chief, New Statesman and Nation; Ronald Hyde, editor, Evening Standard; Gerard Berry, editor, New Chronicle;

Action resulting from my mission and—no doubt—other reports:

On December 7, 1942, two weeks after I began reporting, Polish National Council passed a resolution dealing with the Jewish extermination and committing the government to act without any delay. (The text of public record).

Three days later, on December 10, 1942, Polish government issued a formal appeal to the Allied governments concerning the extermination of the Jews in Poland.

On December 17, 1942, the Allied Council (representatives of all Allied governments) unnanimously passed a public Appeal of the Allied Nations in behalf of the Jews.

Two days later, on December 19, 1942, President of the Polish Republic sent a note to Pope Pius XII asking for intervention in behalf of the Jews. (The text reproduced in numerous publication—after the war).

Then, one month later, on January 18, 1943, Polish Foreign Minister, Edward Raczynski presented his government's demands in behalf of the Polish Jews at the Allied Nation's Council; bombing of Germany as reprisals for the continued extermination of the Jews; forwarding demands to Berlin to let the Jews out of the German-dominated countries; demanding action as to make the Allied as well as neutral countries accept the Jews, who succeeded or would succeed in leaving the German-dominated countries.

British Foreign Secretary, Anthony Eden, in the name of H.M. government, rejected all demands, offering vague promises to intervene in some neutral countries. (Minutes of the session eventually became public).

Beginning in March 1943, secret executions of the Polish hoodlums, who acted against the Jews were carried out. The names of the criminals and the nature of their crimes were publicized in the Underground press.

The Directorate of the Civil Resistance which organized Underground courts had been established already in 1942. It was headed again by Korbonski. By the way, he lives just a few blocks away. Last April—36 years after the war ended—he had been decorated by the Israeli Ambassador with a Yad Vashem Medal for the Rightous Among the Nations. I called him to come and listen to my report. He answered that he would love to come—but he was not invited.

In the early 1943 numerous articles, based on my information, appeared in the British press. Public demonstrations had been organized. In May 1943, a pamphlet was published authored by a prominent Soviet writer, Alexey Tolstoy, German writer Thomas Mann and myself (described as a "Polish Underground Worker"). The pamphlet was entitled "The Fate of the Jews."

MY MISSION IN THE USA

In June 1943 at the suggestion of the American Ambassador Biddle, I was sent to Washington, still secretly, under an assumed name, Jan Karski. I stayed there until August 1943, living on the premises of the Embassy. Polish ambassador, Jan Ciechanowski, supervised my activities and organized my contacts.

I reported to the following individuals (only the most important will be mentioned): Franklin Delano Roosevelt, President of the United States; Cordell Hull, Secretary of State; Henry Stimson, Secretary of War; Francis Biddle, Attorney General; Colonel Donovan, chief, Office of Strategic Service (O.S.S.); Apostolic Delegate, Cardinal Ameieto, Giovanni Cicognani; Archbishop Mooney; Archbishop Spelman; Archbishop Strich; Dr. Nahum Goldman, President, American Jewish Congress; Rabbi Stephen Wise, President, World Jewish Congress; Waldman, American Jewish Congress; Felix Frankfurter, Justice of the Supreme Court; and Backer, Joint Distribution Committee. Publishers and commentators: Mrs. Ogden Reed, publisher, New York Herald Tribune; Walter Lippmann; George Sokolsky; Leon Denned, editor, The American Mercury; Eugene Loyons; Dorothy Thompson; William Prescott, The New York Times; and Frederick Kuh, Chicago Sun.

Upon my return to London, Prime Minister Mikolajczyk informed me that he would not send me to Poland for the duration of the war. I saw too many people in the United States and I became too well-known. German radio mentioned my activities in America, describing me, by the way, as a "Bolshevik agent on the payroll of American Jews." My additional shortcoming—as he explained—were recognizable scars on both my wrists. In June 1940—on my third secret expedition—I was captured by Gestapo in Preshov, Slovakia. Unable to withstand torture, I tried to commit suicide, cutting my veins with a concealed blade. It did not work. Transported to Poland for further interrogation, I had been rescued by the Underground. But, even after a cosmic operation, the scars remained. Gestapo certainly had my files and I became a public figure, he argued.

Two months later, in October 1943, I was sent to the United States—for the second time but openly and again as Karski—to speak, write, report, inform the public-at-large—openly.

Since October 1943, until the end of the war, I delivered some 200 lectures in the United States: from coast to coast: from Rhode Island to Florida. In all of them I spoke about the Jewish tradegy. Every lecture had been reviewed in the local press.

Then came my articles on what the Jews demanded, on what I saw in Warsaw ghetto and Belsec in Colliers; New York Times; The American Mercury; La France Libre; The Jewish Forum; Common Cause; Herald Tribune; New Europe; Harper's Bazaar. Many of them had been illustrated—several under my personal supervision. Various exhibitions has been organized.

Then, in 1944—still during the war, I published a book, Story of a Secret State. Its central theme was my visits to the Warsaw ghetto and Belsec. The book became Book-of-the-Month Club Selection. Soon after it was published in Great Britain, Sweden, Switzerland, France.

Many of you gave testimony on the Jewish Gehenna. Respect is due to you. The Lord assigned me a role to speak and write during the war, when—as it seemed to me—it might help. It did not.

Later, however, when the war came to its end, I learned that the governments, the leaders, scholars, writers did not know what had been happening to the Jews. They were taken by surprise. The murder of six million innocents was a secret. A "Terrible Secret" as Laqueur reports.

Then, I became a Jew. Like the family of my wife, who is sitting in this audience—all of them perished in the ghettos, concentration camps, gas chambers—so, all murdered Jews became my family.

But I am a Christian Jew. I am a practicing Catholic. And, although not a heretic, still my faith tells me the Second Original Sin had been committed by humanity: through commission, or omission, or self-imposed ignorance, or insensitivity, or self-interest, or hypocrisy, or heartless rationalisation.

This sin will haunt humanity to the end of time.

It does haunt me. And I want it to be so.

When Professor Karski referred to the fact that Stefan Korbonski, whom he had mentioned several times in his report as an active participant in the defense of the Jews in Poland, lived only a few blocks away from the State Department but was not invited to the conference, cries of outrage broke out among those present. Elie Wiesel responded by spreading his arms in a gesture of helplessness. Such were his thanks for the scores of messages about the Holocaust in progress, sent regularly to

London at the risk of the lives of the Polish radio operators, hunted mercilessly by Nazi detection squads.

Shoah

The Poles watching in the United States on the television screen the four installments of *Shoah*, ten hours in all, could easily come to the conclusion that it was an anti-Polish film. Its author, the French Jew Lanzmann, focused attention on the Poles, making them the witnesses of the Holocaust, providing the background of the action, together with shots of a bleak, depressing Polish landscape.

The Holocaust witnesses interviewed by Lanzmann after forty years were old and decrepit, visibly intimidated by the television camera. Lanzmann did not approach them in a friendly manner, but rather as a prosecutor asking inquisitorial questions and exerting psychological pressure. Skillful editing left on the screen only replies which could be interpreted as expressing indifference, presenting the Poles as anti-Semites with no sympathy for the victims. The film emphasized an episode in which a young boy driving a horse cart, when asked by the Jews in a train where they were going, responded by a gesture of passing his hand over his throat, meaning that they were doomed. Lanzmann calls it "a purely sadistic gesture," without offering any alternative answer which the boy could have given in the presence of the German guards. The warning he conveyed might have allowed at least some of the Jews to escape. The Polish witnesses were haggard, toothless wrecks in rags. They were obviously selected to project an image, though there must still be many witnesses of the Holocaust who are in their fifties, and are not derelicts. Lanzmann showed repeatedly the same railroad track, the same locomotive and driver, the same dismal scenery and miserable shacks. This did not add much to the film's value but conveyed a suggestion of passive inaction reflecting the alleged indifference of Poles, which bordered on complicity. There was not a hint of the powerful Polish resistance and the stubborn struggle against the Nazi invaders.

Shoah was received with bitter resentment by the Polish American community. The Polish American Congress, representing the millions of Americans of Polish descent, issued an official response to the hostile propaganda promoted by Lanzmann:

SHOAH: A BIASED ACCOUNT OF THE HOLOCAUST

Reinforces the Prejudiced Stereotype of Polish Anti-Semitism
Statement by the Polish American Congress Executive Committee

Polish Americans are concerned that *Shoah* presents a narrow, one-sided view of the Polish people as anti-Semites, to a degree which hardly distinguishes them from the German Nazis.

Shoah is Claude Lanzmann's personal account of the Holocaust—a masterly work of art—but at the same time a cunning distortion of the truth, designed to justify his preconceived notion of the Poles' complicity in the extermination of Jews by the Germans during World War II. To a question posed in an interview by the French *L'Express* (May 1985) whether the film "is an act of accusation against Poland," Lanzmann replied. "Yes, it is the Poles who accuse themselves. They mastered the routine of extermination." Thus, *Shoah* must not be considered a definitive, historical documentary. This is the point on which we are most sensitive: that, based on *Shoah*, the viewer will form an unfair perception about the Poles and people of Polish heritage.

Shoah presents the story of the Jewish Holocaust totally detached from the terror instituted by the Germans in occupied Europe, especially in Poland, where 3 million Christian Poles were brutally murdered in street executions, Nazi prisons and concentration camps, alongside the 6 million European Jews exterminated within the German program of the "final solution."

While the Jewish Holocaust is unique—in that the Jews were marked for extermination solely because they were Jews—the 3 million Christian Poles were murdered in a comparable effort designed to annihilate Polish intelligentsia and leaders so that Poles would be reduced to the level of subhuman slave labor for the German Reich.

Understandably, Polish Americans are concerned that *Shoah* might be erroneously regarded as the definitive history of those times of unconceivable horror. We feel that the film is unfair because it does not reflect the efforts of Poles to help Jews to survive. It must be remembered that only in Poland was any help accorded to the Jews puinishable by death, not only of the person who rendered assistance, but also of his entire family and, in some cases, of an entire village.

Despite this, approximately one third of the 6,000 Righteous Gentiles commemorated at the Yad Vashem Memorial in Israel for the heroic saving of Jewish lives are Poles. Failure to include these aspects of Polish suffering and Polish aid to the Jews implies that Polish people were uniformly passive in the fact of the Holocaust and even cooperated with the Germans in the extermination of the Jews. Errors and omissions in the translation from Polish to French to English tend to reinforce this implication.

Beneath the callousness and indifference of the Poles to the tragic fate of the Jews—as alleged in *Shoah*—lies the stereotype of the "endemic anti-Semitism of Poles" presented in several books, articles and TV productions. Anti-Semitism was a fact of life in Europe and in the United States as well as in prewar Poland, especially in the 1930's, stemming from the religious, social and cultural differences and the disparity of the two communities. There must be no apology for it. It was a social evil which must be condemned and fought.

" . . . on the eve of World War II, the Jews in Poland numbered some three-and-a-half million people out of total population . . . of only about thirty-four million. . . . This mass of Jews was able through the centuries to develop their own society and their own culture. Their freedom to pursue traditional faith in peace and to cultivate an autonomous way of life affecting education, language, dress and even the administration of justice enabled them to cohere into one of the greatest Jewish communities of all time," reminded Harold B. Segel, director of the Columbia University Institute on East Central Europe in a paper presented at the 1983 conference on "Poles and Jews: Myth and Reality in the Historical Context." "To argue that this occured *despite* the Poles, or in the face of Polish *hostility*, or *Polish repression*, would be to ignore the evidence of numbers," he commented.

During the past several years, Polish Americans and Jewish Americans have been engaged in a dialog designed to bring about a closer understanding of the tragedy of both peoples leading to a mutual trust and cooperation. We are concerned that, through its tendentious accusations, generalizations and distortions of historical facts, *Shoah* does a grave disservice to both communities in that it tends to polarize them in their often misguided perceptions of their mutual history and prevents cooperation in their common interest. We must not allow this to happen.

For the POLISH AMERICAN CONGRESS:
Aloysius A. Mazewski, President
Helen Zielinski, Vice President
Kazimierz Lukomski, Vice President
Bernard B. Rogalski, Secretary General
Edward G. Dykla, Treasurer

SHOAH

Jan Karski, Ph.D.

At the beginning of last October, I was invited to a private showing of the movie *Shoah*. The movie lasted more than nine hours. It has no actors and limits itself to interviews with victims of the Holocaust, its perpetrators and eyewitnesses. Also shown are original German documents and reports. There are many contemporary photographs taken by Germans. Some of the interviews (with Germans) are filmed surreptitiously. In addition, the camps, crematoria, neighboring villages and towns are shown as they appeared during the war and as they appear today. The movie's director is a Frenchman, Claude Lanzmann. He filmed in Poland, Czechoslovakia, Greece, Holland, Israel, Switzerland, Rumania, as well as the United States. He devoted a dozen years of his life to this work.

Shoah is unquestionably the greatest movie about the tragedy of the Jews which has appeared after the war. No one has managed to present the destruction of the Jews during World War II in such depth, with such bloodcurdling brutality and lack of mercy for the viewer. At the same time, the interweaving of people, events, nature and time is full of bewitching poetry. The soothing beauty of the trees grown over the places of slaughter; the country sod and fields, covering the terrible secrets of the concentration camps; a procession exiting a church which served as a round-up point for deported Jews; the moving prayers in a synagogue of those who lived; an old woman who survived and sings a Jewish song "from those times"—all this shocks with dread or captivates with beauty and innocence.

The Pope learned of *Shoah* and praised the movie and conscientiousness of its creator to an audience of French and Belgian war veterans. He also underscored the moral significance of the movie. The Pope's remarks appeared in the September 27 issue of *Osservatore Romano*.

The subject of the movie is the torment and eventual extermination of defenseless Jews, including three million Poles practicing Judaism or of Jewish ancestry. Nothing more. The movie does not portray the background of the war years, the conquering of almost all of Europe by the Third Reich and the horrors carried out against the subjugated peoples. It does not speak about the suffering of the non-Jewish population of Poland, Russia, Greece or Serbia. The rigorous construction of the movie does not allow for this.

Lanzmann's intention is to demonstrate to the viewer that the Jewish Holocaust was *unique* and *incomparable*. He is unquestionably right. To equate the extermination of the Jews with the suffering and losses of the non-Jewish population in Europe is, after all, although emotionally understandable, simply spiritless. All nations had victims to a greater or lesser extent. But ALL Jews were victims. This Lanzmann does not forget for even a moment. Every viewer of this movie will understand this.

The uncompromising restriction of the topic creates an impression that the Jews were abandoned by all mankind, that all mankind was insensitive to their fate. This is, however, untrue and disheartening, particularly for postwar and future generations of Jews. The Jews were abandoned by governments, by those who had the physical or spiritual power. They were not abandoned by mankind. After all, several hundred thousand Jews were saved in Europe. In Poland, tens of thousands survived. The penalty for harboring a Jew in Poland was death. In Western Europe, although the punishment was not as extreme, helping or harboring Jews exposed people to great dangers, Nevertheless, millions of peasants, workers, intellectuals, priests, nuns, endangering themselves and their relatives, provided aid to Jews in each country of Europe. How many of them perished? God only knows.

In Poland, a clandestine organization was created whose sole objective was to provide haven and aid to hiding Jews. Its head Wladyslaw Bartoszewski lives in Warsaw. Marek Edelman, one of the heroic leaders of the Warsaw Ghetto uprising, lives in Lodz. Jan Nowak and Jerzy Lerski, two couriers of the Polish underground government, now living in the United States, carried messages and pleas from Jewish leaders in Poland to Western governments. Stefan Korbonski, the last chief of the Polish Underground State and like Lerski a recipient of the "Righteous Among Nations" award, now lives in Washington, D.C. Others live in other countries. They should at least be mentioned. The viewer should be made to realize, particularly the young generation of Jews and non-Jews, that such people existed, and this, it seems to me, is necessary regardless of the movie's construction. For some it is necessary so that they do not lose faith in mankind and their place within mankind—for others, so that they understand what a lack of tolerance, racism, anti-Semitism and hatred lead to and what love of neighbor can do. This is more important than any construction, particularly since this is such a great movie and will have such an impact on the viewer.

The movie's technique rests on interviews, some planned and some happenstance with individual[s] not known to Lanzmann. In this second group are remarks of several Poles, residents of towns and villages adjacent to the camps. Some attest to sympathy and kindness of heart, most apall. For instance, some small town peasant women, when asked what they think of the destruction of the Jews, answer that they live better than before. They took over homes left by the Jews which were grander than those in which they had lived before the war. A peasant woman from another group, although not asked, lectures Lanzmann that the fate which the Jews met was God's punishment for handing over the Savior to his death. She makes these statements just before a religious procession and the church in the background. Apparently the teachings of the Second Vatican Council describing such views as sinful have not yet reached this parish.

An educated urban resident, without being asked, leaves a crowd to run before the movie camera in order to inform Lanzmann about what a friend had supposedly witnessed. A rabbi was explaining to the Jews gathered for deportation that their fate was due to the actions of their ancestors who delivering Christ to His death cried out that His blood would fall on them and their offspring. He did not say that the Jews and the rabbi were surrounded by SS-men with revolvers and nightsticks in their hands.

An old farmer questioned if he is sorry that there are no more Jews answers with a smile, yes and no. When he was young he liked Jewish women. Now he is old and indifferent. Another Polish peasant from around Treblinka describes the transport of Jews from Western Europe which he claims to have observed. At the last trainstop prior to Treblinka, Pullman wagons pulled up. They were occupied by fat Jews and Jewish women with fancy hairdos. Inside the wagons were tables with bottles of perfumes. He saw suitcases with gold. At the stop, one of the Jews left the wagon and walked up to the station buffet in order to buy something. The doors to the wagons were not guarded. He was allowed to get out—just before Treblinka. Dear God, how absurd!

The movie includes an interview with me. The circumstrances surrounding the interview speak to the methods employed by Lanzmann and the planned parameters of *Shoah*. He visited me in 1977 providing me with materials attesting to his qualifications, previous movies, etc. He talked about his project. He had heard and read about me. He indicated it was my duty to agree to an interview. Initially, I refused. I had walked away from my war experiences and for more than thirty years I did not return to those memories. Finally, I agreed, requesting written questions. I wanted to prepare. He refused. He did not want prepared answers. He would ask about those matters that belong in the movie. I would say what I remembered. I agreed, with the *caveat* that he

not try to enmesh me in political discussions, assessments of con-
clusions. He answered that in no way did that lie in his intentions.

The interview took place at my house in 1978. He filmed for two
days, in total about eight hours. Lanzmann is a difficult person. Pas-
sionate. Completely devoted to his work. Uncompromising in his questioning and establishing of facts. A few times I broke down emotionally.
Once he broke down. My wife, unable to bear it, left the house.

From the eight hours of filming, I saw about forty minutes of the
interview on the screen, focussing on the suffering of the Jews in the
Warsaw Ghetto as well as the desperate demands for assistance from
the underground Jewish leaders aimed at the Western governments. I
understood. The time devoted to my account and the construction of
Shoah forced Lanzmann to omit the section of the interview which I felt
was the most important part of my Jewish mission at the end of 1942.

As a courier of the Polish Underground State, who had personally
witnessed beginnings of the final solution, I was sent to alarm the
Western world to the fate of the European Jews under the Nazi occupation. The suffering of the Jews was described by others in the movie for
more than seven hours. Many did it better than I. For me, the central
point of my interview was that having made my way to the West, I
described the tragedy and demands of the Jews to four members of the
British War Cabinet including Eden; President Roosevelt and three key
members of the American government; the Apostolic Delegate in Washington; Jewish leaders in the United States; distinguished writers and
political commentators such as Walter Lippmann and George Sokolsky.
None of these matters could be discussed by anyone else. After all, this
would have demonstrated how the allied governments, which alone
were capable of providing assistance to the Jews, left the Jews to their
own fate.

Including this material into the movie, as well as general information
about those who attempted to help the Jews, would have presented the
Holocaust in a historically more accurate perspective. The leaders of
nations, powerful governments either decided about the extermination
or took part in the extermination or acted indifferently toward the
extermination. People, ordinary people, millions of people sym-
pathized with the Jews or provided assistance.

The movie *Shoah* through its greatness of talent, determination and
fierce truth, but also by its self-limitation, has created the need for the
next movie, equally great, equally truthful—a movie which will present
a second reality of the Holocaust. Governments, social organizations,
churches, people of talent and heart should find a form of cooperative
effort in order to produce such a movie. Not in order to contradict that
which *Shoah* shows but to complement it. After all, the Jewish Holocaust of the Second World War weighs on all of mankind like a curse.

POLAND ON TRIAL—*SHOAH*
Kazimierz Lukomski

Shoah is undoubtedly a most convincing—in its stark brutality—film depicting the drama of the extermination of the Jews by the Germans during World War II. It bears witness to a tragedy unprecedented in the annals of human history—the tragedy of the six million European Jews condemned to die a slow, agonizing death in the gas chambers of the extermination camps established by the Germans in occupied Poland, *only* because they were Jews. The Jewish Holocaust is unique and incomparable. It cannot be equated with the death, persecution and suffering inflicted by the Germans on all peoples conquered by them, even considering the three million Polish dead. No one should forget this.

Shoah documents the extermination of the Jews in a devastatingly frank manner. Unfortunately, it is presented with the total exclusion of the realities of the German conquest and occupation of practically all of Europe. It is as if the Jewish Holocaust constituted the only dramatic event in wartime Europe. The result is in fact a distortion of the history of the period.

Thus, according to director Claude Lanzmann, the only reaction of the Polish people to the tragedy of the Jews was at best an equivocal snicker. Did it mask just callousness and insensitivity? Or smug satisfaction that once the Jews disappear from Polish villages and towns, the Poles would move to their better homes? The message is there . . . not stated, but clearly and intentionally implied.

In Lanzmann's film, Poles manned the trains which delivered human cargo to Oswiecim, Treblinka. . . . They knew the fate of the victims. Polish peasants worked their fields a hundred yards from the camps. They knew what was going on behind the barbed wire. They heard the screams. They continued plowing their fields. "At first, it was unbearable. Then you got used to it," recounts a villager. Unmoved and unconcerned. So also were the villagers in Grabow.

Six days before the final German attack on the remnants of the Warsaw Ghetto in April, 1943, Mordecai Anielewicz, commander of the Jewish Combat Organization, asked Polish Underground leaders to arm the Jews. "They refused," related Itzhak Zuckerman, JCO second-in-command. Period. Unmoved and unconcerned.

According to Lanzmann, there was not a single Pole who in any way helped, or even tried to help, the Jews, with the possible exception of Jan Karski, a courier from the Polish Underground to the Polish Government-in-Exile, who in the Fall of 1942 attempted to alarm Western leaders to the fate of the Jews in occupied Eruope. He tried. He described the tragedy to members of the British war cabinet, including

Foreign Secretary Anthony Eden, President Roosevelt and members of the United States Government, Jewish leaders in the United States, including Supreme Court Justice Felix Frankfurter and Rabbi Stephen Wise. All to no avail. They refused to believe his story. No action was taken by the Western allies hiding behind the formula of "rescue through victory"—obviously too late. (Also see Walter Laquer's *The Terrible Secret.*)

Lanzmann omitted that part of Karski's interview, presenting in *Shoah* only Karski's heart-rendering description of conditions in the Ghetto, which he visited prior to leaving Poland on his way to the West. It would not fit Lanzmann's central objective: "a broad indictment of Polish Catholic callousness, if not complicity, in the Nazi killing of millions of Jews." (Gabe Fuentis, *Chicago Tribune,* January 13, 1986) The Parisian daily *Liberation* headlined its extensive review of *Shoah* even more bluntly: **Poland on Trial.**

It is Lanzmann's arbitrary selection of interviewees and their skilful and purposeful questioning that seemingly achieve this objective without *j'accuse* ever actually being uttered. Of the 350 hours of taped interviews, Mr. Lanzmann used in *Shoah* only 9½. Clearly, conformance to his preconceived thesis of "Polish Catholic callousness, if not complicity" in the extermination of Jews by the Germans, determined his selection of footage.

Thus his treatment of the Ghetto Uprising and the alleged Polish refusal to help the JCO fighters, as related in *Shoah* by Itzhak Zuckerman . . . "They refused," he claimed. There is no need to question Mr. Zuckerman's recollection of those traumatic events 40 years ago. But, in fact, the Poles did deliver a small quantity of arms (of the limited amount they had) and, further, the Polish Home Army (AK) attempted on two separate occasions to break into the Ghetto to assist and relieve the Jewish fighters. Both times they were repelled by the Germans with heavy casualties inflicted on the Poles. Mr. Lanzmann must have been aware of this since he interviewed another of the JCO leaders, now living in Poland, *Solidarnosc* activist Mark Edelman. He chose to ignore it.

The Polish Underground's limited assistance to the JCO heroic fighters must be evaluated in a larger context. Even if it may sound callous, the Ghetto Uprising, following three years of the Jews' virtually passive submission to German extermination policies, did not have a chance. It was doomed, whatever assistance Poles would have provided. A larger Polish effort could only have prolonged the agony by a few days, while significantly disrupting preparedness for an all-out effort to liberate Poland from the shackles of German terror. As it was, at the outbreak of the Warsaw Uprising just over one year later, only some 10% of the Home Army fighters were actually armed. Hard choices. . . But those were hard times.

Beneath the callousness and indifference of the Poles to the tragic fate of the Jews, as alleged in *Shoah*, lies the stereotype of the "endemic anti-Semitism of Poles" prevalent among the large and vocal segments of Jewish Americans. There was anti-Semitism in Poland, just as there was—and still exists—anti-Semitism in practically all countries with a significant Jewish minority. The Jewish population in Poland constituted a tightly-knit community, in its mass leading a life largely separated from the Poles by its distinctive and strictly observed religion, tradition, culture and customs. Almost strangers among the native Poles, the situation was understandably not conducive to truly good, neighborly relations. Juxtaposed on a Jewish share of an estimated 30% of the Polish national income, it did evoke a degree of resentment, i.e., anti-Semitism.

In evaluating the centuries of Jewish domicile in Poland, one has to balance the ugly manifestations of anti-Semitism with the prevailing climate, which helped create a substantial, distinctive Jewish culture emanating far beyond the borders of Poland. Prior to World War II, the Jewish community in Poland numbered 3,300,000, 12% of Poland's population. Jewish intellectuals, businessmen and professional people played a significant role in the affairs of the nation. In 1937, some 250 periodicals and over 700 books were published in Poland by its Jewish community. These conditions existed in spite of the fact that the 1930's did witness a rise of anti-Semitism, which manifested itself in efforts to enforce segregation at some universities, economic boycotts to reduce Jewish preponderance in commerce, and yes, violence, limited loss of life and destruction of some Jewish property. Such, very briefly, is the record—neither uniformly pretty nor entirely ugly. It is a very complex story, which requires close, dispassionate examination, free of emotionalism and preconceived prejudice . . . on both sides.

Mr. Lanzmann claims that there was not a single Pole who helped the Jews. I submit the Polish efforts to save the Jews surpassed anything in other countries occupied by the Germans. It is mainly through these efforts that some 100,000 Jews survived the Holocaust, hidden in Polish homes and Catholic monasteries and assisted in numerous other ways. Several thousand Poles were engaged in these efforts, even though only in Poland was any form of assistance to the Jews punishable by death. No one will ever know how many Poles were executed.

In his tendentious presentation, Mr. Lanzmann follows the regrettably familiar pattern of accusations levelled against the Poles. Thus, speaking of the Holocaust to Boston students, Mr. Elie Wiesel, one of the top leaders of American Jews, is quoted in the *Boston Globe* (April 23, 1985) as saying: "Please, it should not become an element that would bring you, move you to hate the Poles, the Hungarians or the Germans for what they have done." In that order!. . . Similarly, Poles are absent in Mr. Wiesel's article, "The Brave Christians Who Saved the Jews from the Nazis," *TV Guide* (April 6, 1985). While he names several people who helped save the Jews, an Austrian, a Bulgarian, a Dutchman, etc., he conveniently ignores the over 2,000 Poles honored at Yad Vashem for helping save the Jews. He further discusses at some length efforts to save Jews undertaken in several countries. Not in Poland. "Are Danes better human beings than Poles?" he asks. In the context of his story, the readers' perception is obvious: yes, the Danes are better human beings than the Poles.

Neither Mr. Lanzmann's account nor Mr. Wiesel's account makes mention of any Poles helping to save the Jews in their hour of agony. That is simply not true. It hurts. It exacerbates resentment. It is devisive.

REMARKS
Kazimierz Lukomski, Vice President, Polish American Congress
at a Press Conference on January 27, 1986 sponsored by
The American Foundation for Polish-Jewish Studies, Inc.

The statement being released today represents an effort by members of the Chicago Polish American—Jewish American Dialogue to break the syndrome of divisiveness and tensions which over the past decades characterized relations between the two communities, overshadowing occasional cooperation in matters of mutual concern. It is the result of an understanding arrived at by a group of leaders of both, that much of the problem is based on misconceptions, held very rigidly about each other, and an inability to listen to each other's experiences and feelings which the traumatic events of World War II evoked. We recognized that the only way to overcome this is through an honest and dispassionate, if often painful, appraisal of the very complex nature of Polish-Jewish experiences.

Throughout, Polish Americans were very conscious of the vociferous accusations of Poles as being virulently anti-Semitic, to the extent that they were willing accomplices of the Germans in their extermination of Jews during World War II, which were leveled in several books, publications and TV productions. Indeed, the anti-Polish chorus helped produce the stereotype of the endemic anti-Semitism of Poles, one expression of which is the widely used by the media, but totally false and insulting, reference to German extermination camps as "Polish death camps."

Poles—Polish Americans were resentful. In some, it induced anti-Jewish sentiments, even where there were none before. Mutual prejudices and recriminations were rampant.

Then came *Shoah* which in some reviews was perceived as a "broad indictment of Polish Catholic callousness, if not complicity, in the Nazi killing of millions of Jews" (Gabe Fuentis, *Chicago Tribune*, January 13, 1986), while the Parisian daily *Liberation* headlined its review even more bluntly: *Poland on Trial.*

Shoah brought the tensions between the Polish American and the Jewish American communities to a head. For too long, faced with the barrage of anti-Polish accusations, the Polish Americans had remained silent. It was time to respond.

In a statement issued in February 1986, the Polish American Congress denounced Claude Lanzmann's film as a "one-sided, deliberately distorted and, as such, an inaccurate and slanted record" of the most devastating event of modern history." It presents the story of the Jewish Holocaust totally detached from the terror concurrently instituted by the Germans in occupied Europe, especially in Poland, whereby 3 million Christian Poles were brutally murdered in street executions, Nazi prisons and concentration camps, alongside the 6 million European Jews exterminated within the program of the 'final solution'," the PAC statement said.

Thus, we became aware of the urgent necessity to break the vicious circle of mutual recriminations and to try to understand and accept the admittedly divergent perceptions of the very complex nature of Polish—Jewish relations in their historical context, and thus to develop our relationship and cooperation in the combined effort to advance the cause of human rights and dignity.

The statement of the Chicago Polish American—Jewish American Dialogue represents an attempt to do just that. It is not intended as a definitive evaluation of Polish—Jewish history. It is designed to diffuse tensions and lower the often acrimonious rhetoric and thus promote cooperation in the areas of mutual interest.

I fully expect the statement will be severely criticized by some in both communities. I feel confident, however, that further discussions and future developments of our relationship will prove the critics wrong.

THE AMERICAN FOUNDATION FOR POLISH-JEWISH STUDIES

Statement of the Chicago Polish American-Jewish American Dialogue around the Film *Shoah*

When publicity for the film *Shoah* appeared in Chicago in December 1985, there was concern that it could induce feelings of tension between the Jewish and Polish American communities. Recognizing this, a group of leaders of the American Jewish committee and a group of prominent Polish Americans, including leaders of the Polish American Congress, agreed to view the film together and begin a dialogue flowing from their shared experience. What follows is the statement of the dialogue participants concerning that endeavor.

* * *

We felt a dialogue was essential to maintain open channels of communication between our two groups, as well as to discuss individual and group perceptions of the film. Jewish and Polish Americans have supported each other in the past on matters of special concern to their respective communities. We wished to continue this spirit of cooperation.

Our dialogue focused on the feelings that *Shoah* aroused in the participants and on the issues it raised. By telling each other our experiences, we developed empathy for each other. Each group was able to restate the feelings of the other, thereby demonstrating that we heard and understood each other.

The Polish Americans expressed compassion for the Jewish grief and profound sense of loss over the systematic annihilation of 6,000,000 of their people. They also recognized that the Jewish experience in the Holocaust was unique—that Jews were marked for extermination solely because they were Jews. They shared the anger which the Jewish participants expressed at the pervasiveness and brutality of the Nazi atrocities. They understood the indignation the Jews felt at the indifference to these events and the abandonment of their people by leaders of allied nations and others in positions of power and authority.

They heard the resentment Jewish Americans expressed at the extent and nature of Eastern European anti-Semitism. They understood the anger the Jews felt that some Poles in the film, who witnessed the horror of the Holocaust, still display traditional anti-Semitic attitudes today.

The Jewish Americans, in turn, expressed compassion toward the Polish Americans' sense of grief and loss over the death of 3,000,000 non-Jewish Poles at the hands of Nazis. Many perished in the same death camps as the Jews. The two groups were united in their indignation at the Nazis' policy of racism, as well as at German programs designed to wipe out Polish intellectuals and leaders so that Poles could surivive only as subhuman slave labor for the German Reich.

The Jewish Americans came to understand the Polish concern and anger that *Shoah* might erroneously be regarded as the definitive history of those times of inconceivable horror. Poles felt the film was unfair because it did not reflect efforts made by some Poles to help Jews survive. The group was reminded that only in Poland was helping a Jew punishable not only by the death of the person who rendered assistance but by the death of his parents and children.

Despite this, approximately one third of the 6,000 righteous Gentiles commemorated at the Yad Vashem Memorial in Israel for heroic saving of Jewish lives are Poles. The Polish Americans felt that, by failing to include these aspects of Polish suffering and Polish aid to Jews, the film implied that the Polish people were uniformly passive in the face of the Holocaust and cooperated with the Germans in the extermination of the Jews. Errors and omissions in the translations of Polish tended to reinforce this implication.

We did not attempt to reconcile our different perceptions of history. These perceptions diverge over the extent of anti-Semitism in Poland. We did agree that anti-Semitism existed in Poland before, during and even after the Nazi occupation. We found it indisputable, however, that such anti-Semitism was not universal and was and is opposed and condemned by some circles of Polish society.

Collectively, we recognized that it is not always possible for Polish Americans and Jewish Americans to agree on what the facts are or what they mean, but that it is wrong to stereotype, to assume that all Poles are anti-Semitic and to assign to Poles universal guilt. In fact, the Jewish Americans welcomed the conviction with which the Polish Americans condemned anti-Semitism wherever it might appear.

We intend to continue working together on those areas on which we agree, such as: combatting anti-Semitism and anti-Polish stereotypes; promoting human rights and democratic freedoms for the people of Poland and for Soviet Jews, including the right of Soviet Jews to practice their faith and to emigrate; promoting commemorations of the Holocaust in its proper historical perspective; bringing Nazi war criminals to justice; supporting generous immigration policies in this country; assuring a haven for Polish asylum seekers and working for the preservation of the State of Israel.

We must send a clear, credible message to our communities about the value of our relationship. The basis on which the groups relate to each other is the experience and vision of a pluralistic America. America's open environment has allowed us to move beyond the troubled past. Accordingly, we will continue to promote and expand the environment for dialogue and cooperation in combined efforts to advance the cause of human rights, dignity and mutual understanding. The way to build our future in America is together.

SIGNATORIES

JERRY BIEDERMAN
Past President, Chicago Chapter,
   The American Jewish
   Committee

EDWIN CUDECKI (deceased)
Former Vice President,
   Copernicus Foundation;
   Former Chairperson, Illinois
   Ethnic Consultation

HOWARD GILBERT
Chairman, National Jewish
    Communal Affairs
    Commission, The American
    Jewish Committee

SHARON GREENBURG
Member, Executive Board,
    Chicago Chapter, The
    American Jewish Committee

MATHILDA JAKUBOWSKI
Commissioner, Illinois
    Commission on Human
    Relations

MITCHELL KOBELINSKI
President, Chicago Chapter,
    American Foundation for
    Polish-Jewish Studies;
    President, Copernicus
    Foundation

JOHN KULCZYCKI, PH.D.
Associate Professor of History,
    University of Illinois at Chicago

MARCIA E. LAZAR
President, Chicago Chapter, The
    American Jewish Committee;
    Vice President, Chicago
    Chapter, American Foundation
    for Polish-Jewish Studies

JONATHAN LEVINE
Midwest Regional Director, The
    American Jewish Committee

KAZIMIERZ LUKOMSKI
National Vice President, Polish
    American Congress

LUCYNA MIGALA
Vice President and Program
    Director, WCEV Radio; Artistic
    Director and General Manager,
    Lira Singers

REV. JOHN T. PAWLIKOWSKI
Professor of Social Ethics,
    Catholic Theological Union;
    Member, U.S. Holocaust
    Memorial Council

ALDERMAN ROMAN
    PUCINSKI
President, Polish American
    Congress Illinois Division

DAVID G. ROTH
National Ethnic Liaison, The
    American Jewish Committee

RABBI HERMAN E.
    SCHAALMAN
Past National President, Central
    Conference of American Rabbis
    Vice President, Chicago
    Chapter, The American Jewish
    Committee

ESTA G. STAR
Vice President and Chairperson,
    Interreligious Affairs
    Commission, Chicago Chapter,
    The American Jewish
    Committee

EWA TRZCINSKA-MEYERHOFF,
    D.D.S.
Vice President, Chicago Chapter,
    Kosciuszko Foundation

WOJCIECH WIERZEWSKI, PH.D.
Editor, Polish National Alliance ZGODA

MAYNARD I. WISHNER
Honorary President, The

American Jewish Committee; Past Chairman, Jewish Committee; Past Chairman, Jewish Community Relations Council of the Jewish United Fund of Metropolitan Chicago

APPENDIX

Events of the past weeks have shown that, in order to escape evacuation, Jews are leaving small Jewish communities. These Jews must have found shelter with Poles. Please advise immediately all city and county executives to inform residents of their communities that every Pole who harbors a Jew becomes guilty. . . This includes even those Poles who may not give Jews shelter but lend them some other form of aid or sell them food. In all such instances these Poles are subject to the death penalty.

The above excerpt from a 1942 internal German communique in occupied Poland demonstrates most vividly the risks taken by those persons who lent any form of assistance to Jews. In no other occupied nation nor in the Third Reich itself was there an official death penalty for helping Jews.

It would be impossible to establish exactly how many Poles were successful in helping Jews to escape the Nazi terror and how many paid with their lives for coming to the aid of Jews in occupied Poland. Most often these were murdered along with those they were trying to rescue, with their families, wives, children, parents, even neighbors. It was not uncommon for the Germans to murder an entire village, then set it aflame, or bury the victims in one common grave.

The following list gives a representative sampling of eyewitness reports of Poles who paid with their lives for rescue actions on behalf of the Jews in occupied Poland. It is truly a chronicle of death. . .

7.IX.1939, Mordarka—Germans executed a Limanow postman along with 9 Jews on whose behalf he tried to intervene.

X. 1940, Lancut—Germans executed Aniela Koziol along with the Wolken-feld family whom she was harboring.

19.XI.1940, Warsaw—Germans murdered a Pole as he threw a sack of bread over the walls of the Warsaw ghetto.

IV.1942, Mlawa—During a Gestapo-organized public execution of 50 Jews, one of the Poles in the crowd started shouting "They are spilling innocent blood." He was immediately seized and murdered along with the Jewish victims.

8.V.1942, Sobujew—Germans executed Jan Machulski for harboring Jews, who managed to escape.

20.V.1942, Czarny Dunajec—Karol Chraca was executed for providing food to Jozef Lehrer and his daughter; the three were buried in a common grave in the Jewish cemetery.

3.VII.1942, Warsaw—Polish Socialists Tadeusz Koral and Ferdynand Grzesik were arrested for teaching tactics of diversion and sabotage in the Ghetto; Koral executed, Grzesik sent to a concentration camp.

21.VII.1942, Warsaw—University of Poznan professor Franciszek Raszeja, a prominent surgeon, was murdered along with Jewish doctors in the Ghetto while administering aid to a Jewish patient.

6.X.1942, Bidaczow Nowy—22 farmers were executed for harboring Jews; they were buried at the scene of the crime in a common grave.

25.X.1942, Poreba—Zofia Wojcik, along with her two children, ages 2–3, were executed along with the Jewish man she was harboring.

XI.1942, Oborki—22 families, the entire population of this village were murdered for giving aid to Jews; only 2 persons survived. The village was burned and the ashes plowed under.

4.XII.1942, Przeworsk—6 persons were executed as a punishment for the aid given to several Jews by the townspeople.

6.XII.1942, Ciepielow Stary near Kielce—SS men burned alive 3 families (21 persons), including 15 children, on suspicion of harboring Jews, for the purpose of frightening the local population—not far away another Polish family hid Jews in their loft until the end of the war. . .

1942, Nowy Sacz—18 year old Stefan Kielbasa was executed for providing a Jewish friend with false "Arian" papers.

1942, Warsaw—For bringing aid and weapons to the Jews in the Ghetto, Zdzislaw Grecki of the Underground Scouting Organization "Szare Szeregi" was publicly shot while his friend was tortured in the Pawiak prison and then executed.

15.1.1943, Pilica-Zamek—German gendarmes executed Maria Rogozinska with her 1 year old son for harboring Jews; they also shot the local guard for not reporting the presence of Jews in his village.

20.11.1943, Lwow—University of Lwow professor Kazimierz Kolbuszewski died after being sent to Majdanek and tortured for harboring one of his Jewish students.

4.VII.1943, Bor Kunowski—43 persons were burned alive in a barn for aiding a unit of partisans, composed mainly of Jews escaped from the Ghetto.

X.1943, Warsaw—Father Roman Archutowski, rector of the Catholic seminary, was sent to Majdanek, where he died after being tortured for helping Jews.

1943, Stryj—Gestapo executed by public hanging a local schoolteacher and his wife for harboring a Jewish family.

II.1944, Sasow—For bringing aid to about 100 Jews hiding in local forests, Germans murdered and/or burned alive everyone in the village, standing guard so that no one escaped the flaming inferno.

VIII.1944, Warsaw—8 Catholic nuns were murdered for harboring Jews in their shelter.

During the expulsion of Jews from Jaslo, at the head of the column were Polish peasants who had harbored and helped Jews; they were also sent off to extermination camps.

Gemans murdered 1000 Poles in Belzec near Lwow for aiding Jews.

Recommended reading:

Abramsky, Cheimen, Maciej Jachimczyk, and Antony Polonsky, Eds. *The Jews in Poland*. Oxford and New York: Basil Blackwell, Ltd., 1986.

Bartoszewski, Wladyslaw and Zofia Lewin. *Righteous Among Nations* London: Earls Court Publications, Ltd., 1969.

Bartoszewski,Wladyslaw and Zofia Lewin. *The Samaritans: Heroes of the Holocaust*. New York: Twin Publishers, Inc., 1970.

Friedman, Philip. *Their Brothers' Keepers*. New York: Holocaust Library, 1978.

Iranek-Osmecki, Kazimierz. *He Who Saves One Life*. New York: Crown Publishers, Inc., 1971.

Laqueur, Walter, *The Terrible Secret*. Boston: Little, Brown, and Co., 1980.

Lukas, Richard C. *Forgotten Holocaust, The Poles under German Occupation, 1938–1944.* Lexington: The University of Kentucky Press, 1986.

Shatyn, Bruno. *A Private War.* Detroit: Wayne State University Press, 1985.

Tec, Nechama. *Christian Rescue of Jews in Nazi-Occupied Poland.* New York: Oxford University Press, 1985.

Appendix

Biography of Stefan Korbonski

STEFAN KORBONSKI was born at Praszka, in Poland in 1903. Still a school student in December 1918, he volunteered for the Polish army, took part in the defense of Lwow against the Ukrainians, and then went back to school. In 1920, during the Polish-Russian war, he enlisted again and in 1921 fought against the Germans in the Silesian uprising. On leaving the army he studied law at Poznan University, joined the Polish Peasant Party in 1925, and in 1929 set up in practice as a lawyer in Warsaw. Continuing his political activities, he was elected in 1936 chairman of the Peasant Party in the Bialystok province.

In 1939 Mr. Korbonski served as lieutenant in the Polish army. He was taken prisoner by the Russian troops but escaped and returned to Warsaw where he helped to organize the Polish Underground Movement. He became a member of the Political Coordinating Committee which directed the entire Polish underground fight against the Germans.

In 1941 he was appointed chief of the Civil Resistance. In this capacity he organized underground courts which condemned about two hundred traitors, Gestapo agents, etc., to death and these sentences were carried out. He established radio communication with the Polish Government in Exile in London, organized the sabotage in production, transport, agriculture and the action of the resistance of the Polish nation.

During the Warsaw Uprising in 1944 he was appointed Secretary of the Interior in the underground government and in March 1945 acting underground Deputy Prime Minister and Delegate in Poland of the London Polish government. Mr. Stefan Korbonski carried out the duties of Chief of the Polish Underground State until his arrest by the Soviet NKVD on June 28, 1945.

After the formation of the Polish so-called Government of National Unity, he was released from prison. He was then elected chairman of the Warsaw District of the Polish Peasant Party and after the general election held on January 19, 1947, he became a member of parliament for the city of Warsaw. He then joined the Executive Committee of the Polish Peasant Party.

In October 1947, when it became apparent that he would be arrested for a second time because of his anti-communist activity, he and his wife, Zofia, fled from Warsaw. On the 5th of November 1947 they managed to escape to Sweden by boat and reached the United States on November 26, 1947.

At present Mr. Korbonski is Chairman of the Polish Council of Unity in the United States, and Chairman of the Polish Delegation to the Assembly of Captive European Nations [ACEN]. He was elected Chairman of the ACEN eight times.

In 1973 Mr. Korbonski received the Alfred Jurzykowski Foundation Award in Literature.

Mr. Korbonski, who is a member of the Polish Institute of Arts and Sciences and of the International Pen Club in Exile, is the author of the following books:

Fighting Warsaw, first edition, Macmillan Company, New York, 1956, and George Allen & Unwin, London, 1956. Second edition, Funk & Wagnalls, New York, 1968.

Warsaw in Chains, Macmillan Company, New York, 1959, and George Allen & Unwin, London, 1966.

Between the Hammer and the Anvil, Hippocrene Books, Inc. New York, 1981.

Polish Underground State—a Guide to the Underground, 1939–1945, Columbia University Press 1978, & Hippocrene Books, Inc., New York 1981.

Mr. Korbonski has the following Polish military decorations: 1. Virtuti Military Cross, 2. Medal for the War of 1920 against Soviet Russia, 3. Silesia Uprising Cross of Valor, 4. Underground Home Army Cross, 5. Medal for the War of 1939–1944, 6. Golden Cross of Merit, American Legion—Medal of Valor.

On June 12, 1980 Yad Vashem Martyrs' and Heroes' Remembrance Authority in Jerusalem conferred upon Mr. Stefan Korbonski a medal of honor for saving Jews during World War II in Nazi occupied Poland.

Articles of Special Interest

These two articles have appeared in 1987 in Poland in *Krytyka,* an underground periodical. Adam Michnik is Poland's best known dissident, and an author of many articles and books, including *Letters from Prison* published in 1987 by the University of California Press.

THE POISONED SOUL OF THE NATION
Wiktor Kulerski

Contemporary Polish anti-Semitism is a painful and shameful disease, a denaturalization of our life as a society, and a curse inflicted on us by the most unfortunate (for us) nineteenth century.

The negative developments in the relationship between the Poles and the Jews in the past seem to resemble the relationships between the Poles and other national minorities, and even between the various classes of society. Was the Polish Republic more anti-Semitic than anti-Ukrainian or anti-peasant?

A number of interrelated developments changed the situation in the nineteenth century when a large part of the "szlachta" (land owning nobility) became "declasse" and impoverished and had to find employment in the villages and the towns. The peasants also began to migrate in search of new ways of earning a living. At the same time the Jewish minority, or Polish Jews whose families had lived in Poland for generations and felt Polish as well as Jewish, who lived in the villages and towns, came under the domination of Russian Jews who migrated en masse into the areas of the former Polish Republic where they came to find a new life. This influx of the Russian Jews was caused by a succession of laws promulgated by tsarist Russia which made it impossible for the Jews to live anywhere in the vast empire except for a designated zone where they could settle. This zone was set up in the newly conquered western territories of the empire, which was, for the most part, the area of the former Polish Republic.

The Polish Jews, at first most antagonistic to the newcomers, finally succumbed to the overwhelming majority. (This antagonism resulted in many fratricidal acts during the 1863 Polish uprising against the Russians when Polish Jews fighting as rebels clashed with the newly arrived Russian Jews who collaborated with the tsarist army). During the nineteenth century the Jewish minority exceeded 10% of the population of that region. Settling as they did, mainly in villages and towns, they became a majority. That percentage of Jewish minority thus exceeded the level above which many ethnic minorities, in various countries, began to be perceived as threatening. This unleashed hostile reactions and even outright aggression on the part of the majority. The massive immigration of the Jews made them the target of antagonism of the local population which saw in the Jews a direct threat to their own interests. The pogroms, inspired by the tsarist regime, only magnified and consolidated that hostility.

The competition with Russian Jews, well acquainted with the conditions of tsarist Russia, and loyal to it, was not easy. A failure could thus be easily blamed on the Jew. To uphold one's own status—often an illusion—to repair one's own damaged dignity, one could also say: "At least I am not a Jew, not one of those who crucified Christ and rejected His teachings, as the Church says." In time, the National Democratic Party supplied many compensatory complexes of ideology, individual and collective. That ideological anti-Semitism of the ND Party, particularly in its National Radical Fraction, gave rise to what Jozef Pilsudski called "the poisoning of the nation's soul."

To the Jews who survived the German Holocaust, communism appeared to be the new Covenant. The mirage of internationalism and of a classless society, gave new hope to that martyred and scattered nation or, what was left of it, as it did to many troubled people. The more afflicted by fate, the easier it was to be taken in by the mirage, and to become its believers. Those were the people, Jews among them, who suffered the most bitter disappointment. The system which was to succor the humbled and the oppressed brought about a new wave of discrimination and privation. It was not only the Jews who succumbed to the siren call of communism. They were not its only victims, but in Poland they got the blame for its evil.

Today, in the eighties, nearly a half century after the Holocaust, the last Polish Jews live among us. Like the last Polish Tartars, and other small national minorities, the Jews are a living testimony to the ancient Polish Republic of many nations and many faiths. Yet our attitude, or the attitude of a sizeable part of Polish nation, towards the last Polish Jews and to the memory of their perished nation, does not bring credit to the proud traditions of the old Republic. To see and to understand what constituted our guilt in the time of the Holocaust, our guilt by omission, as Jan Blonski described it in his splendid article, the responsiblity for our reaction to the German Holocaust as Kazimierz Wyka wrote, to see and to understand that responsibility one does not have to delve in the archives of the past.

Still today, a half century after that Holocaust, Polish high school graduates, celebrating Christmas Eve, can still draw on the backboard, behind the back of a Jewish colleague, the star of David hanging from the gallows. Still today, little children playing in the yard can chase away a kid with the hateful, cruel call "Jewboy" or "Jewgirl." In the streetcars and buses one can hear epithets similar and worse, usually without any reaction from the fellow passengers. One can even hear such sentiments: "Hitler deserves a monument for what he did to the Jews even though he failed to do the job properly since there are still some left. No matter, we'll finish them someday." In quite a few localities where the Jews perished, the memorial tablets were vandalized and desecrated, as happened in Anin and Rembertow. Still today none other than attorney Sila Nowicki can hold forth that the Jews of today carry 1% of the blood of those who crucified Christ. In at least two respected Warsaw churches you can buy new editions of the notorious "Protocols of the Wise Men of Zion" commissioned at one time by the tsarist Ochrana, not to mention other anti-Semitic periodicals and lectures. I know priests who explain to the faithful that individual words and gestures of John Paul II towards the Jews are only a tactical and political necessity. Finally, here and now, the Minister of the Interior, speaking in the Sejm, can publicly and explicitly pick on the Jewish origin of citizens who have served Poland with distinction and been persecuted as well.

What more can we say? It will not help us to cover up such facts with an old and threadbare curtain, woven from the examples of our sacrifices and generosity in saving Jews from the German Holocaust. Such conduct cannot cure our progressive disease. This can only be done by facing the truth about ourselves, the truth that we shall proclaim, loud and clear, to ourselves and to those to whom we owe it. Only then, purified by the truth, the time may come when Polish Jews, those who live with us, and those scattered throughout the world, may be able to say: "I am a Polish Jew" and we can say: I am a Pole" without pain, in peace and with a serene heart.

—"Krytyka" #25 1987. Translated by Jacek Galazka

THE PERSISTENT TEMPTATION OF THE TRUTH
Adam Michnik

I) My friend Wiktor Kulerski has written a pro-Semitic article. That he felt the need to do so clearly proves that the problem of anti-Semitism deserves reflection. Pro-Semitism is always a reaction to anti-Semitism much as, let's say, pro-Polonism is always the result of persecutions which afflict the Polish nation. These are reactions born of a noble moral impulse, but they remain moral reactions.

Before I dispute his position, I consider it appropriate to remind the reader of my origins. It is not, I believe, a consideration important to me, but, it may be important to some readers. I am a Pole of Jewish origin which I emphasize only when I speak on subjects related to anti-Semitism. W. Kulerski has provoked these comments by statements which I consider one sided, and thus incorrect and misleading. It is not the soul of the nation that is poisoned. It is the soul of the anti-Semite that is poisoned.

I do not find the term "Polish anti-Semitism" acceptable. I prefer to speak of anti-Semitism which occurs among Poles. The difference is real. Anti-Semitism is not a specific characteristic of the Polish nation, but a way of thinking in some circles in various countries. There are anti-Semites in Russia, France, England and Czechoslovakia. They are also in Poland. The condemnation of anti-Semitism should not in any specific way be aimed at the Polish nation which has a wide range of attitudes in this matter.

II) Did the Jews support communism? An overwhelming majority of communists of Jewish origin did not identify themselves with the Jewish nation. They saw themselves as Poles, or, simply as communists. Berman and Minc, mentioned so often in anti-Semitic arguments, were culturally totally polonized while politically they identifed themselves with Soviet Russia. To the Jewish community they were renegades who had abandoned the language, religion and national identity of their fathers. To call them "Jews" makes as much sense as calling the Hitlerite and Soviet generals bearing Polish names, "Polish."

III) The argument of Wiktor Kulerski pleases me because of its sympathy for the Jagiellonian idea—the idea of Poland of many nations, languages and religions. Such multiplicity gives birth to a sense of unity of a higher order, to universal values and cultural wealth. Yet, multiplicity gives birth to conflicts as well. In the years of the Second Republic [1918–1938—translator] on both the Polish and the Jewish sides there existed a wide spectrum of attitudes, open and closed, universalist and xenophoboic, tolerant and poisoned by chauvinism. Anti-Semitism was an element in some circles. What is more, by the way, speaking of "Polish anti-Semitism" camouflages the real anti-Semites and shifts the blame onto the entire Polish nation. In fact, the responsibility for anti-Semitic excesses rests on anti-Semites. They, not the Polish nation, should be held to account for their anti-Semitism. Whoever says that all Poles are responsible for anti-Semitism, absolves all the anti-Semites of that accusation, since he, who is responsible for everything, is responsible for nothing.

IV) This applies to an even greater degree to the theories of the Polish passivity in the face of the annihilation of the Jews. Such an accusation used to come up as proof of the statement that the Poles were guilty of complicity in the crime of genocide. This totally absurd accusation permitted Western public opinion to accept the betrayal of Poland at Yalta. After all, the nation which lent its hand to the horror of Treblinka—doesn't it deserve the Soviet communism?

Yet it is difficult to accuse even the anti-Semites, those who declared their anti-Semitism clearly and openly, of such complicity. The Poles did not collaborate with the Nazis in the destruction of the Jews, or, in any other matter. Individual collaborators were condemned to death and quite a few of them were executed by the underground. No one has the right to accuse anyone, who, facing the brutal terror of the Nazi occupation, was afraid to save the Jews because he feared for his life and the lives of his family. Those who did perform such acts of heroism deserve the highest respect and admiration, but, their attitude cannot be considered a norm. Heroism can never be the norm.

But, let us add that notorious anti-Semites cannot use the heroism of such people as an alibi. There were anti-Semitic attitudes in the Polish underground fighting the Germans. Even a cursory reading of the rightist underground press testifies to that. I consider it correct and important that such facts should be revealed and calmly analyzed. Accusing the Polish nation of a "cover up" is false and pointless. This path leads to a dead-end, hiding real anti-Semites, and to the false temptation of the righteous to admit to sins they did not commit. Those who have never been anti-Semites have no need to plead publicly "mea culpa."

V) Wiktor Kulerski relates a number of events which, in his opinion, constitute current examples of anti-Semitism in Poland. I could equally relate as many facts illustrating the existence of pro-Semitic attitudes. What do they prove? Not much, I am afraid. Just as it does not prove much when Wladyslaw Sila-Nowicki (for many years a political prisoner of the Stalin era, a most effective defense counsel in political trials, a brave soldier of the Polish Underground Army and a true Polish patriot) wrote an unwise article in which he repeated a number of current arguments from the anti-Semitic repertoire. It also does not prove anything that two churches are selling anti-Semitic pamphlets. There are, after all, more than two churches in Poland. In another church, on the anniversary of the Warsaw Ghetto Uprising, a Catholic priest publicly confessed to the sin of anti-Semitism among Poles. It is difficult to ignore the wide publicity given to the visit of the Pope to a synagogue, and to forget the fact that the church was the only place where in the summer of 1986 the victims of the [1946] Kielce pogrom were commemorated. How can one forget that anti-Semitism is most sharply condemned in Catholic publications?

What do these facts prove? They prove that the subject is very complicated. They also mean that the dispute about anti-Semitism in a land devoid of Jews is not a dispute about the attitude towards Jews, but, to the world at large, about a Polish cultural paradigm, about Polish ethics and the definition of Polish national dignity. This dispute goes on within the Polish nation and the Church. It goes on to decide whether Poland is to be tolerant and open to diversity or a xenophobic backwater; deliberately pluralistic or forcibly standardized; an element of democratic Europe or a poor relation locked into a narrow chauvinistic obscurantism.

The attitude towards anti-Semitism is the litmus paper in this dispute. Whatever the anti-Semites might say on this subject does not relate to the attitude towards the Jews.

In Poland there are no Jews and they will never return. The anti-Semites want to give vent to their frustration and to articulate their own irrationality. Most of all they want to build a national unity on the emotion of a national complex and tribal hate.

In this dispute I am with my friend Wiktor Kulerski on condition that he will reject pro-Semitism in favor of sober judgment and will not burden the Polish nation with the blame which attaches exclusively to Polish xenophobes. Each one of us has too many of our own sins to answer also for the sins of others. Let us leave the sin of anti-Semitism to the anti-Semites, so that in their declarations they cannot use the name of Poland in vain. Let them have no occasion to defend the good name of the Poles. Let them defend only the bad name of their anti-Semitic aberration.

"Krytyka" #25 1987 Translated by Jacek Galazka

Index